◆

Grow Rich
with the
Power *of* Your
Subconscious
Mind

◆

Grow Rich

with the

Power *of* Your

Subconscious

Mind

◆

JOSEPH MURPHY

A TarcherPerigee Book

an imprint of Penguin Random House LLC

penguinrandomhouse.com

Copyright © 2020 by D-Strategy

Compilation revisions and new text copyright © 2020 by D-Strategy
with permission of the Trust

Original text by Dr. Joseph Murphy

Most TarcherPerigee books are available at special quantity discounts for bulk
purchase for sales promotions, premiums, fund-raising, and educational needs.
Special books or book excerpts also can be created to fit specific needs. For
details, write: SpecialMarkets@penguinrandomhouse.com.

Library of Congress Cataloging-in-Publication Data
Names: Murphy, Joseph, 1898–1981, author.
Title: Grow rich with the power of your subconscious mind / Joseph Murphy.
Description: New York: TarcherPerigee, Penguin Random House LLC, 2020.
Identifiers: LCCN 2020032934 (print) | LCCN 2020032935 (ebook) |
ISBN 9780593192078 (hardcover) | ISBN 9780593192085 (ebook)
Subjects: LCSH: Success in business. | Success. |
Mental discipline. | Subconsciousness.
Classification: LCC HF5386 .M8568 2020 (print) |
LCC HF5386 (ebook) | DDC 332.024/01—dc23
LC record available at https://lccn.loc.gov/2020032934
LC ebook record available at https://lccn.loc.gov/2020032935

Printed in the United States of America
1   3   5   7   9   10   8   6   4   2

Book design by Lorie Pagnozzi

Contents

✦

CHAPTER 14
Affirmations for Health, Wealth, Relationships, and Self-Fulfillment 191

Preface

◆

Grow Rich with the Power of Your Subconscious Mind sounds like a proposition too good to be true. In fact, Dr. Joseph Murphy, the author of this book, specifically *discourages* readers from putting great effort into pursuing riches and other objects of desire. Only "effortless effort" is required. The only effort needed involves learning how to project your desires onto the screen of your subconscious mind in such a way that you envision yourself being, doing, or having that which you desire, whatever it may be. When you develop this ability, the Omnipotent Cosmic Power within you, which permeates all beings, finds the means to fulfill your desire.

Keep in mind that the concept of "effortless effort" applies exclusively to the pursuit of one's desires and not to how one lives one's life. Each person's goal in life is self-fulfillment, which necessitates making conscious use of our minds and bodies and often requires effort and determination. When we follow our passions and are aligned with Omnipotent Cosmic Power, the work required may feel effortless, but at times, we may struggle. Tenacity and hard work may be required to power through those difficult times and overcome any obstacles.

Rest assured, however, that whatever image you successfully imprint on your subconscious mind is ultimately reflected in the real world. In other words, your experiences and circumstances are the product of whatever you think and truly believe. As Murphy explains, this principle can be a blessing or a curse. Just as images of health, wealth, and happiness can be impressed upon the subconscious mind, so too can images of illness, poverty, and sorrow. For example, negative self-talk, such as "I'll never be able to afford that," when passed to the subconscious, is made manifest in the real world. Likewise, fear of illness, failure, or rejection, when it becomes a subconscious belief in the subjective mind, becomes an objective reality in the world.

To change your experiences, circumstances, and financial status, you must change your thinking and beliefs. Unfortunately, this is easier said than done. One must take a "leap of faith." Merely saying that you think or believe or want something to be so does not make it a belief; merely repeating an affirmation falls short of impressing the desire on the subconscious mind. The image must be burned onto the subconscious with the heat of positive emotion—desire, expectancy, gratitude, and so on. Likewise, negative emotions, such as fear and anxiety, must be discharged to prevent them from projecting false and self-defeating beliefs onto the subconscious.

What makes this book so valuable is that it shows you how to take your leap of faith in baby steps. Murphy was a chemist, a philosopher, a teacher, and a minister in the *New Thought movement*—a school of thought based on the Cosmic Power of the mind to achieve health, prosperity, peace, and personal fulfillment. Murphy authored a number of popular books, including *The Power of Your Subconscious Mind* and *The Cosmic Power Within You*. He believed that all individuals, regardless of education and training, have divine powers and the right to know how to use these powers to fulfill all their desires. As such, he was committed to unlocking ancient secrets and translating often obscure metaphysical concepts and practices into plain English to make them more accessible to anyone who is eager to learn.

In this new volume, you will find some of Dr. Murphy's most powerful writings on the subject of attaining prosperity. Some of the writings appeared in pamphlets distributed at speaking events and have never before appeared in book form, while others have previously appeared in books. (For more on his life and career, see the About the Author section at the end of this book.) This new volume has also been updated throughout for contemporary readers. Among other updates, you'll find a few modern-day examples (which appear in italics) and the addition of content that extends Murphy's teachings on the subconscious to conscious thought and action.

Murphy's philosophy and practices are timeless. Some stories and anecdotes may have resonated more with readers in the 1950s than with today's readers, but they are still relevant and remain effective in illustrating the practical application of Murphy's teachings. In this book, you will find many real-life stories of people who practiced the techniques Murphy recommends and, as a result, attained rich and fulfilling lives. As you dig in and begin to practice these same techniques yourself, you will begin to experience the power of the subconscious mind in your own life. Murphy's explanations of these techniques, along with the many affirmations he provides, make it easy to start using the power of your subconscious mind to enrich your life today.

Although Murphy wrote and taught in the 1950s to the late

1970s and you may encounter an occasional anachronism, the heart of his teachings seem to be even more relevant in today's world, where negativity, chronic illness, misfortune, and poverty seem to prevail. Murphy teaches that we can transcend the uncertain, ever-changing world around us, which he refers to as the "five-sense world," and turn inward to the unchanging and everlasting power within us, where peace, prosperity, and goodness reign. The principles on which Murphy's teachings and techniques are based are eternal; they predate all religions and religious groups and do not rely on external circumstances. When we master these eternal principles, we are unmoved by the negativity of the mass mind and the ups and downs in the world around us.

As you read this book, you may notice that certain terms, such as God, Father, Almighty, I Am, Divine Being, Supreme Being, Infinite Power, Cosmic Power, Divine Intelligence, Divine Wisdom, and the like are capitalized. The reason for this is that these terms reference the same intelligent life force that dwells in all things seen and unseen. Regardless of any organized religious beliefs you accept or reject, the deceptively simple eternal truths revealed in this book hold great power, if you can pause to consider them and put them into practice. Divine Being, regardless of what you call It, dwells in you, and when you learn how to align your conscious and subconscious minds with this power, you will begin to leverage it to your advantage, and miracles will start to happen in your life!

As you begin to put Murphy's teachings into practice, be prepared to make major changes in your approach to pursuing wealth, happiness, and self-fulfillment. The biggest change required and the very first step is to change your mind, your thought. As Murphy points out, a change in thinking leads to positive transformation in who you are, what you do, and, ultimately, what you have. Follow Murphy's guidance presented in this book and make major changes to your approach to riches. You will be well on your way to having the wealth you imagine.

Wishing you success,
Dr. H. Boyer, Trustee
Joseph Murphy Trust

What This Book Can Do for You

♦

There is an Infinite Power within you that can lift you up, heal you, inspire you, guide you, direct you, and set you on the freeway to wealth, happiness, freedom, peace of mind, and the joy of fulfilled and triumphant living. Some people have discovered how to tap into this power; they are happy, joyous, successful, and prosperous. Those who haven't yet discovered this power are at the mercy of external circumstances and life's ups and downs; they are often unhappy and frustrated and cannot make ends meet.

Vast numbers of people in all walks of life go forward day by day, achieving and accomplishing great things. They are vital, strong, and healthy, and are contributing countless blessings to humanity. They seem to be imbued or possessed with some primal force that constantly works for their benefit.

Countless others, however, are leading mediocre, dull lives, full of burdens, in quiet desperation. They seem to have an inability to meet triumphantly and victoriously the challenges of life to win its satisfying rewards.

Why You Need This Book

This book teaches you how to meet and overcome the frustrations and problems of life. Each chapter reveals to you that every problem is always divinely outmatched and shows you how to rise victoriously above any problem into the dawn of a new day and a rich and satisfying new life.

This book explains how to tap the Infinite Power within you and supplies you with specific techniques for putting it into operation.

It is for the express purpose of teaching the reader how to align and communicate with this Infinite Power and how to use It in his or her daily life that this book was created. Every page explains the great basic, fundamental, and unlimited powers of the mind in the simplest and most direct language possible.

Study this book sincerely and apply the many effective techniques presented herein. As you do this, your mental contact and communication with this Infinite Power within you will cause you to rise confidently above confusion, misery, melancholy, and failure to obtain all the good things you desire.

This Infinite Power will unerringly guide you to your true place, solve your problems and difficulties, sever you forever from the conditions of lack and limitation, and set you on the road to higher aspects of living life gloriously and serenely.

What the Infinite Powers of the Mind Have Done for Others

Over the course of more than thirty years, countless numbers of people around the world have used the Infinite Powers of their subconscious minds to be, do, and have all they desire:

+ Wealth in great abundance

+ New friends and wonderful companions in life

+ Protection from all danger

+ Healing of so-called incurable maladies

+ Freedom from self-condemnation and self-criticism

+ Public acclaim, honor, and recognition

+ New vitality and a zest for life

+ Marital peace and happiness where discord was

+ Serenity in this changing world

Men, women, and teenagers who have used this Power come from every level of society and from every possible income bracket. They are high school and college students, office workers, taxi drivers, college professors, scientists, pharmacists, bankers, medical doctors, chiropractors, telephone operators, motion picture directors, actresses, and truck drivers.

These people have discovered this mysterious but intensely real Power which lifted them from failure, misery, lack, and despair, and—in many instances "in the twinkling of an eye"—solved their problems, wiped away their tears, cut them free from emotional and financial entanglement, and placed them on the great high road to freedom, fame, fortune, and glorious new opportunities for fulfilled living. These same people discovered a magical healing love which mended their bruised and broken hearts and restored their souls.

The greatest working truths in life are the simplest. This book presents these great truths with simplicity and clarity. It shows you how to rise above any problems you may have, and how to receive guidance and blessings. Simply ask, believing that it will be so, and it will be done. Your subconscious, in concert with the Cosmic Power of Mind, will make it happen.

Every day of your life will become richer, grander, nobler, and more wonderful as you follow the specific techniques presented in this book for releasing this Infinite Hidden Power within you for all good. Follow the instructions and tap this Infinite Power, and you will attract an abundance of all good things in life.

Begin now, using this book to release the imprisoned splendor within you, and let wonders of all that is good and satisfying happen in your life.

Grow Rich

with the

Power *of* Your

Subconscious

Mind

CHAPTER I

Understand How the Subconscious Mind Works to Create Wealth

◆

Your subconscious mind is like a genie in a bottle—whatever you desire and believe true, your subconscious mind will find a way to bring it to fruition. If you desire and believe you will be blessed with good health, prosperity, and fulfilling relationships, you will be. If, on the other hand, you expect or fear illness, poverty, and loneliness, those will be your fate. To get what you want out of life, first you must learn how the subconscious mind functions.

The whole world and all its treasures—the sea, the air, the earth, all living and nonliving things seen and unseen—were here when you were born. Begin to think of the untold and undiscovered riches all around you, waiting for the intelligence to bring them forth. Look at wealth as the air you breathe. Develop that attitude of mind. Ralph Waldo Emerson expressed this succinctly when asked by a woman how she could prosper. He took her down to the ocean and said, "Take a look." She said, "Oh, there's plenty of water, isn't there?" He said, "Look at wealth that way and you'll always have it."

Realize that wealth is like a tide forever flowing out, forever flowing back. A sales manager said to me that an associate of his sold a million-dollar idea for expansion to the organization. You can have an idea worth a fortune, too. Wealth is a thought image in your mind. Wealth is an idea in your mind. Wealth is a mental attitude.

You can have an idea worth a fortune. Moreover, you are here to release the splendor within you and surround yourself with luxury, beauty, and the riches of life. But you must develop the right *attitude* toward money, wealth, food, clothing, travel, and all things good and desirable. When you truly make friends with wealth, you will always have a surplus of it.

Many people mistakenly believe that you can feel wealthy only when you are in possession of riches. However, the contrary is true; you attract riches only when you feel wealthy. Waiting or hoping for money to come your way is a trap. You must take the leap of faith; you must live in expectancy and gratitude of the wealth you imagine before you can begin to attract what you desire.

Look upon money as a divine idea, maintaining the economic health of the nations of the world. When money is circulating freely in your life, you are economically healthy in the same manner as when your blood is circulating freely, you are free from congestion. Begin now to see money in its true significance and role in life as a symbol of exchange. That's all it is. It has taken many forms down through the ages. Money to you should mean freedom from want. It should mean beauty, luxury, abundance, sense of security, and refinement. You are entitled to it. It is normal and natural for you to desire a fuller, richer, happier, and more wonderful life.

Are some people destined or chosen to experience and to enjoy riches of this world, while others are destined to suffer hardship and deprivation? Absolutely not. We define our own destiny. We receive what we think and truly believe and accept is ours to be, to do, and to have. The Divine Power and Presence within us continuously models and fashions the conditions and circumstances of our daily lives according to the conscious thoughts we impress upon our subconscious minds as images, feelings, and beliefs.

Why the Rich Get Richer and the Poor Get Poorer

Those who enjoy the true abundance and prosperity of life are those who are aware of the creative power of mind, thought, and belief. As they continually impress their deeper minds with ideas of spiritual, mental, and material abundance—prosperity and plenty—that deeper mind automatically causes abundance to be objectified in their experience.

This is the great and Divine Law of Life—operative and effective in everyone. This has always and ever will be true. Our deep-seated, heartfelt beliefs become manifest as experiences, events, and conditions. They become objectified experience—in accordance with the nature of our ideations.

If we are aware and convinced that we are alive in a generous, intelligent, infinitely productive universe—given and governed by a loving Force or a Cosmic Power—our conviction will be reflected in our circumstances and activities.

Likewise, if my dominant conviction is, "I am not worthy of infinite universal wealth," that I'm doomed or fated to remain without, that wealth is for others but not me, then this conviction will be reflected in my circumstances and activities.

These two opposing concepts or beliefs are the primary determinants of whether we are rich in material abundance, or poor. Thoughts of abundance produce abundance; thoughts of lack produce lack. That is why "the rich get richer and the poor get poorer."

Disciplined Thinking

I know thinking of abundance and wealth when you are poor requires some doing. I also know it can be done. It requires sustained and continuous belief that it will come to pass. The person who practices this disciplined thinking will inevitably achieve wealth.

The key phrase is "disciplined thinking." Discipline of the mind begins when we are eager, willing, yearning for Truth. It requires no more and no less than that we examine and understand our heartfelt beliefs, opinions, ideals, and aspirations. This, too, is within the realm of possibility. We must renew our mind, think in a new way.

A young woman, a very good writer who had had several articles accepted for publication, said to me, "I don't write for money." I said to her, "What's wrong with money?" It's true you don't write for money, but labor is worthy of its hire. What you write inspires, lifts up, and encourages others. When you adopt the right attitude, financial compensation will automatically come to you freely and copiously.

She actually disliked money. Once she referred to money as "filthy lucre," going back, I suppose, to the early days when she heard her mother or somebody say that money is evil, or that the love of money is the root of all evil, all these things without any understanding at all. It's a rank superstition to say money is evil or to refer to it as filthy lucre. This woman had a subconscious pattern that there was some virtue in poverty. There isn't. I explained to her that there was no evil in the universe—that good and evil were in the thoughts and motivations of people. All evil comes from misinterpretations of life and misuse of the laws of mind.

If you want money, be friendly with money and you will never lack it. When money is in circulation, times are prosperous. When people begin to brood and worry, fear—the ugly monster—raises its head and a depression or recession sets in. It is all purely psychological. There is no shortage in nature. Nature is lavish, extravagant, and bountiful. It has been said that the amount of fruit that falls to the ground and rots in the tropics every year would feed the whole world. Shortages are due to abuse of nature's bounty and our failures in distribution.

The only evil is ignorance; the only consequence is suffering. It would be foolish to pronounce gold, platinum, silver, nickel, or copper evil. How absurd, grotesque, and stupid that is. The only difference between one substance and another is the number and rate of motions of electrons revolving around the central nucleus.

To overcome her irrational hatred of money, this woman practiced a simple technique, which multiplied wealth in her experience; she repeated the following affirmation daily:

> My writings go forth to bless, heal, inspire, elevate, and dignify the minds and hearts of men and women. I am divinely compensated in a wonderful way. I look upon money as Divine Substance, for everything is made from the One Spirit. I know matter and Spirit are one. Money is constantly circulating in my

life, and I use it wisely and constructively. **Money flows to me freely, joyously, and endlessly. Money is an idea in the mind of the Divine. It is good and very good.**

That's a wonderful affirmation. It eradicates that superstitious nonsense about money being evil and that there is some virtue in poverty, or that God loves the poor more than He loves the rich. This young lady's changed attitude toward money has worked wonders in her life. Her income has tripled in three months, which was just the beginning of her financial prosperity. Such a change in attitude toward money can work similar wonders in your life, too.

Some years ago, I talked with a clergyman who had a very good following. He had an excellent knowledge of the laws of mind and was able to impart this knowledge to others. But he could never make ends meet. He had what he thought was a good alibi for his plight by quoting "Money is the root of all evil," forgetting that the Omnipotent gives riches to people so they can help others. People are encouraged to place their trust or faith in the Intelligent Life Force that gives us richly all things to enjoy.

Love is to give your allegiance, loyalty, and faith to the Source of all things, which is the Living Spirit or the Life Principle in you. You are not, therefore, to give your allegiance, loyalty, and trust to created things, but to the Creator, the Eternal Source of everything in the universe, the Source of your own breath, the Source of your life, the Source of the hair on your head, the Source of your heartbeat, the Source of the sun and the moon and the stars, the Source of the world and the earth you walk on.

If you say, "All I want is money, nothing else, nothing but money matters," you can get it, of course, but you are here to lead a balanced life. You must also claim peace, harmony, beauty, guidance, love, joy, and wholeness in all aspects of your life. How can you live without courage, faith, love, goodwill, and joy in this world today? There is nothing wrong with money, not a thing in the world, but that's not the sole aim in life. To make money the sole aim in life would constitute an error, a wrong choice. There wouldn't be anything evil in it, but you would be imbalanced and lopsided.

You must express your hidden talents. You must find your true place in life. You must experience the joy of contributing to the growth, happiness, and success of others. We are all here to give. Give of your talents to the world. The All Powerful gave you everything, including the Divine Power within you. You have a tremendous debt to pay, because you owe everything you have to the Infinite; therefore, you are here to give life and love and truth to your ideals, your dreams, and your aspirations. You are here to row the boat, put your hands on the wheel, and contribute to the success and happiness not only of your children but also of the world.

To accumulate money to the exclusion of everything else causes one to become imbalanced, lopsided, and frustrated. Yes, as you apply the laws of your subconscious in the right way, you can have all the money you want and still have peace of mind, harmony, wholeness, and serenity. You can do a lot of good with it. You can use it wisely, judiciously, and constructively, like anything in nature. You can use your knowledge, your philosophy in a constructive way, or you can begin to brainwash impressionable minds with self-limiting thoughts and beliefs.

I pointed out to this minister how he was completely misinterpreting the scripture in pronouncing metals (coins) or pieces of paper evil, when these were neutral substances, for there is nothing good but thinking makes it so. He began to see all the good he could do with more money for his wife, family, and parishioners. He changed his attitude and let go of his superstition. He began to claim boldly, regularly, and systematically:

> Infinite Spirit reveals better ways for me to serve. I am inspired and illumined from On High, and I give a Divine transfusion, a faith, and confidence in the One presence and power to all those who hear me. I look upon money as a divine idea, and it is constantly circulating in my life and that of all the people who surround me. We use it wisely, judiciously, and constructively under the guidance and wisdom of the Supreme Life Force.

This young clergyman made a habit of this affirmation knowing that it would activate the powers of his subconscious mind. Today he has a beautiful church, which he wanted (the people built it for him). He has a radio program and all the money he needs for his personal, worldly, and cultural needs. I can assure you he no longer criticizes money. If you do, it will fly away from you, because you are condemning that which you desire.

The Four-Step Process

Follow this technique, which I am going to outline for you, and you will never want for wealth all the days of your life, for it is the master key to wealth.

Step 1: Reason it out in your mind that the Life Principle or the Living Spirit is the Source of the universe, the galaxies in space, and everything seen and unseen: the stars in the sky, the mountains, the lakes, the deposits in the earth and the sea, all animals and plants, the air we breathe, and all forces of nature. The Life Principle gave birth to you, and all the powers, qualities, and attributes of this Life Principle are within you. Come to a simple conclusion that everything you see and are aware of came out of the invisible mind of the Infinite, or the Life Principle, and that everything ever invented, created, or made came out of the invisible human mind; and the human mind and the mind of the Divine are one, for there is only one mind. That mind is common to all people. Everyone is an inlet and outlet to all that is.

Come now to a clear-cut decision that the Life Force is the Source of your supply of energy, vitality, health, creative ideas, the Source of the sun, the air you breathe, the apple you eat, and the money in your pocket. For everything is made inside and out of the invisible. It is as easy for the Life Force to become wealth in your life as it is for It to become a blade of grass or a crystal of snow.

Step 2: Decide now to engrave in your subconscious mind the idea of wealth. *Ideas are conveyed to the subconscious by repetition, faith, and expectancy.* By repeating a thought pattern or an act over and over, it becomes automatic; and your subconscious, being compulsive, will be compelled to express wealth. The pattern is the same as learning to walk, swim, play the piano, type, or drive a car. You must believe in what you are affirming. It is not mumbo jumbo; it is not idle affirmation. You must believe in what you are affirming, like you believe that when you plant seeds in the ground they grow after their kind. Whatever you desire and imagine are the seeds deposited in your subconscious mind.

Realize that what you are affirming is like the apple seed you deposit in the ground. They grow after their kind. You can imagine the seed going from your conscious to your subconscious mind and being reproduced on the screen of space. By watering and fertilizing these seeds, you accelerate their growth. Know what you are doing and why you are doing it. You are writing it with your conscious pen to your subconscious mind, because you know wealth exists and is yours to claim.

Step 3: Repeat the following affirmation for about five minutes night and morning:

> I am now writing to my subconscious mind the idea of Divine Wealth. The Life Force is the Source of my supply, and I know It is the Life Principle within me, and I know I am alive. All my needs are met at every moment of time and point of space. Divine Wealth flows freely, joyously, and ceaselessly into my experience, and I give thanks for the riches forever circulating in my experience.

Step 4: When thoughts of lack come to you, such as, "I can't afford that trip," or "I can't pay my mortgage," or "I can't afford this bill," replace them with thoughts of wealth and prosperity. Never, never let a negative statement about finances go unchallenged. This is mandatory. Reverse it immediately in your mind by affirming, "The Life Force is my instant and everlasting supply, and that bill is paid in Divine Order." If a negative thought comes to you fifty times in one hour, reverse it each time by thinking and affirming, "Divine Power is my instant supply, meeting that need right now." After a while the thought of financial lack will lose all momentum, and you will find your subconscious is being conditioned to wealth. If you look at a new car, for example, never say,

"I can't buy that" or "I can't afford it." Your subconscious takes you literally and blocks all your good. On the contrary, say to yourself, "That car is for sale. It is a Divine Idea, and I accept it in Divine Order through Divine Love." This is the master key to wealth.

Follow this four-step process to set the law of opulence in operation. It will work for you as well as for anybody else. The law of mind applies to everyone, regardless of race, creed, or status. Your thoughts, accepted in faith, make you wealthy or poor. Choose the riches of life right here and right now.

From Failure to Success

A sales manager referred one of his staff to me for counseling. This sales representative was a brilliant college graduate. He knew his products very well. He was in a lucrative territory but was making only $30,000 annually in commissions. The sales manager felt he should double or triple it. In talking with the young man, I found he was down on himself. He had developed a subconscious pattern or self-image of $30,000 a year. In other words, "that's all I am worth." He said that he had been born in a poverty-stricken home and that his parents had told him he was destined to be poor. His stepfather had always told him, "You will never amount to anything. You are dumb, you are stupid." These thoughts were accepted by his impressionable mind, and he was experiencing his subconscious belief in lack and limitation.

I explained to him that he could change his subconscious mind by feeding it with life-giving patterns. Accordingly, I gave him a simple spiritual formula to follow, which would transform his life. I explained to him that he should under no circumstances deny what he affirmed, because his subconscious mind accepted what he really believed.

He affirmed every morning before going to work:

> I am born to succeed. I am born to win. The Infinite within me can't fail. Divine Law and Order govern my life. Divine Peace fills my soul. Divine Love saturates my mind. Infinite Intelligence guides me in all ways. Divine Riches flow to me freely, joyously, endlessly, and ceaselessly. I am advancing, moving forward, and growing mentally, spiritually, financially, and in all other ways. I know these truths are sinking into my subconscious mind, and I know and believe they will grow after their kind.

A few years later when I met this young man again, I discovered that he had been transformed. He said, "I am appreciating life now and wonderful things have happened. I have an income of $150,000 this year, five times greater than the previous year." He has learned the simple truth: that whatever he inscribes on his subconscious mind becomes effective and functional in his life. That power is within you. You can use it also.

Wealth Is an Idea

I recently met a man who used to work in a bank. He was earning $60,000 a year, which was quite satisfactory, but he wanted to make more money for his wife and children. He made a practice of affirming, "The All Powerful is my instant supply. I am divinely guided in all ways. Infinite Spirit opens up a new door." He told me that an opportunity came to him some months ago and that he now is working in sales on a commission basis. He had enough faith in himself to leave the secure bank job and move on. He is now earning $200,000 a year, all expenses paid. He is able to do great things, and he and his family are enjoying a wonderful life.

All this began as an idea in his mind. Wealth is an idea. A radio is an idea. Television is an idea. An automobile is an idea. Everything around you is an idea made manifest in the world.

Use the following meditation to gain assurance and financial wealth:

> I know that my faith in Divine Power determines my future.
> My faith is in all things good. I unite myself now with true
> ideas, and I know the future will be the image and likeness of
> my habitual thinking. As I think in my heart or subconscious,
> so I will be. From this moment forward my thoughts are on all
> things true, all things honest, all things just, all things lovely
> and of good report. Day and night I meditate on these things,
> and I know these seeds, which are thoughts, which I habitually
> dwell upon, will become a rich harvest for me. I am the captain
> of my soul; I am the master of my fate. For my thought and my
> feeling are my destiny.

Affirmations are not for the purpose of changing the Living Spirit or the Life Principle or for influencing the Divine. This Eternal Force is the same yesterday, today, and forever. You don't change It, but you align yourself mentally with that which was always present. You don't create harmony; harmony is. You don't create love; the Living Spirit is love, and It lives within you. You don't create peace; the Living Spirit is peace, and It dwells within you. But you must claim that the peace of Living Spirit floods your mind. You must claim that the harmony of the Living Spirit is in your home. Harmony is in your pocketbook, your business, and all phases of your life. All good is available to each of us. Our affirmations are for the purpose of bringing our own minds to the point where we can accept the gifts that were given to us from the foundation of time. For the Living Spirit is the giver and the gift.

There is a guiding principle that will lead you: The only place we can cure our lack and limitation is in our own mind. We don't need to work on external conditions; we need only to work on ourselves. Our internal thoughts will manifest as our external conditions.

When we have done it there (in the subconscious mind), we shall find that the world (our health, wealth, and self-fulfillment) will be a mathematical reflection of our inner state of mind. Whatsoever things you envision as you repeat your affirmation, believe that you have received them and you shall have them. That is the basis of Cosmic Power, whether directed toward the healing of our bodies, prosperity, success, achievement, or material benefits. Once you convince your deeper mind that you have what you want, your deeper mind (your subconscious) will proceed to bring it to pass.

You may wonder, "How can I convince my deeper mind, my subconscious, that I have riches or any other good thing when my common sense tells me that bills are piling up, creditors are after me, the bank is demanding payment, and so on?" You can't. If you keep thinking about debts and obligations and how much you owe, you will only magnify your misery. You must disregard the five-sense world and go to the Infinite Power, which dwells within you and communicates with the Divine through your subconscious.

Once your subconscious accepts your statement as fact, it proceeds to do everything possible to bring riches to you. That's the whole purpose of affirmation: so that you convince yourself of the truth of that which you affirm. Then your deeper mind will bring these things to pass.

If you have a lot of debts and obligations, a lot of bills to pay, don't worry about them. Turn to the Source, which is endless. Be like a farmer who focuses on growing a crop and not on the weeds, knowing that a healthy crop will crowd out the weeds, and they will die away. As you focus on your good, on guidance, right action, and the Eternal Source of your supply, thoughts of lack and limitation will die in you, and the Eternal Source will multiply your good exceedingly.

Be Joyful

Joy is feelings of delight, gratitude, and total freedom. When full of joy, a person cannot possibly feel worried, anxious, or uncomfortable, or hold a negative thought. Whatever activity the person is engaged in is effortless. This is the state of mind that is so conducive to attracting riches.

Claim joy by imagining it and affirming it. Joy is the spirit of life, the expression of life. Don't work like a horse at it. No willpower is used in this mental and spiritual therapeutic technique. Just know and claim that joy is flowing through you now, and wonders will happen. Freedom and peace of mind will be yours. If you have peace of mind, you will have peace in your pocketbook, your home, and your relationships with people, for peace is the power at the heart of the Divine.

A woman said to me, "I was blocked financially. I had reached the point where I had not enough money for food for the children. All I had was five dollars. I held it in my hand and said, 'God will multiply this exceedingly according to His riches and glory, and I am now filled with the riches of the Infinite. All my needs are instantaneously met now and all the days of my life.'"

She believed that. Those weren't idle words. You don't gain the ear of the Almighty by vain repetitions. No, you must know what you are doing and why you are doing it. You must know that your conscious mind is a pen and with it you are writing something, engraving something in your subconscious mind. Whatever you impress upon your subconscious mind will be expressed on the screen of space. It will come forth as form, function, experience, and events—good or bad. So, make sure you impress that which is lovely and of good report.

She said, "For about a half hour, I affirmed that all my needs are instantaneously met now and all the days of my life, and a great sense of peace came over me. I spent the five dollars freely for food. The owner of the market asked me if I wanted to work there as a cashier since the present one had just left. I accepted the position and shortly afterward I married the owner, my boss, and we have experienced and are experiencing all the riches of life."

This woman looked to the Source. She didn't know how her directive to her subconscious would be carried out, because you never know the workings of the subconscious. She believed in her heart in the blessings of the Infinite. To believe is to live in the state of being that which you believe and to be alive to the Eternal Truths. Her good was magnified and multiplied exceedingly because the subconscious always magnifies what you give attention to.

There is a Divine Presence and Power within you, and you can use it. You can stir up the gift of this presence and power within you, for It is the giver and the gift; and everything has been given to you. Therefore, you can tune in, claim guidance, right action, beauty, love, peace, abundance, security. You can say to yourself, "Divine Ideas unfold within me, bringing me harmony, health, peace, and joy." If you are in business, if you are in a profession, if you are an artist, if you are an inventor, just sit down quietly and say, "Infinite Intelligence reveals to me new creative ideas, original, wonderful ideas, which bless humanity in countless ways." Then watch the wonderful ideas come to you. And they will come, because when you call, the Infinite Power answers.

The nature of Infinite Intelligence is responsiveness. Call and the response comes. Constantly affirm, feel, and believe that the Living Spirit multiplies your good exceedingly, and you will be enriched every moment of the day spiritually, mentally, intellectually, financially, and socially. For there is no end to the glory of daily living. Watch the wonders that will happen as you impress these truths in your subconscious mind. As you read these words, let these truths sink into your subconscious. They will, and they are. You are engraving them. The more often you do this, the quicker you will transfer your desires to your subconscious, and you will begin to experience a glorious future financially and in every way.

A word of caution: Be careful what you think and discuss. Never talk about economic lack and limitation. Never talk about being poor or in want. It is very foolish to talk to your neighbors or relatives about hard times, financial problems, and like matters. Count your blessings. Begin to think prosperous thoughts. Talk about the

Divine Riches present everywhere. Realize that the feeling of wealth produces wealth. When you talk about not having enough to go around and how little you have and how you must cut corners, these thoughts are creative; and you are only impoverishing yourself. Use money freely. Release it with joy and realize that Divine Wealth flows to you in avalanches of abundance.

Look up to the Source. As you turn to the Divine Presence within you, the response will come. The Cosmic Life Force cares for you. You will find neighbors, strangers, and associates adding to your good and to your supply of material things. Make it a practice to request Divine Guidance in all facets of your life and believe that Supreme Intelligence is supplying all your needs according to Its riches in glory. Claim it boldly. Come boldly to the throne of grace.

Grace is simply the mathematical, orderly reflection of your habitual thinking and imagery. In other words, there is a Supreme Intelligence that responds to your subconscious thinking and imagery. Claim Divine Guidance, therefore, in all aspects of your life. As you make a habit of this attitude of mind, you will find the invisible law of opulence can and will produce visible riches for you.

Recently a doctor told me that her constant affirmation was as follows: "I live in the joyous expectancy of the best, and invariably the best comes to me." She has learned that she is not dependent on people for joy, health, success, happiness, or peace of mind. She looks to the Living Spirit Almighty within her for promotion, achievement, wealth, success, and happiness. Contemplate promotion, success, achievement, illumination, and inspiration, and the spirit of the Almighty will move on your behalf, compelling you to express fully what you meditate on. Let go now and permit the Infinite riches of the Infinite One to open new doors for you and let wonders happen in your life.

Don't Try So Hard

As you claim wealth, avoid struggle and strain. Don't try to force things. How could you add power to omnipotence? Can you make a seed grow? You can't. Plant it in the ground. It will grow. The oak is in the acorn. The apple is in the apple seed. The archetype of pattern is there, but you must deposit it in the soil where it dies, undergoes dissolution, and bequeaths its energy to another form of itself.

When a spiritually minded person looks at an acorn, he sees a forest. That's the way your subconscious works. It magnifies your good exceedingly. So, avoid strain, since this attitude is indicative of your own belief. Worry, fear, and anxiety inhibit your good. They create blocks, delays, and impediments in your life. Whatever you fear will happen to you. Reverse it. Meditate on what you love. Love is an emotional attachment. In your subconscious Love is all the wisdom and power necessary to solve any problem.

Your conscious mind is prone to look at external conditions and tends continually to struggle and resist. Remember, however, it is the quiet mind that gets things done. Quiet your body and mind periodically; tell them to be still and relaxed. When your conscious mind is quiet and receptive, the wisdom of your subconscious rises to the surface mind, and you receive your solution.

A salon operator told me that the secret of her success was that every morning prior to opening the doors, she has a quiet period in which she reflects:

> Divine Peace fills my soul. Divine Love saturates my whole being. Infinite Intelligence guides, prospers, and inspires me. I am illumined from On High. This healing love flows from me to all my clients. Divine Love comes in my door. Divine Love goes out of my door. All those who come into my salon are blessed, healed, and inspired. The infinite healing presence saturates the whole place. This is the day the Lord has made, and I rejoice and give thanks for the countless blessings that come to my clients and me.

She has this affirmation written out on a card and reiterates these truths every morning. At night she gives thanks for all her clients, claiming that they are guided, prosperous, happy, and harmonious and that Divine Love flows through each one filling up all the empty vessels in her life. She stated to me that following this pattern, at the end of three months she had far more clients than she could handle. She had to hire three additional stylists. She discovered the riches of effective affirmation and is prospering beyond her dreams.

Trust Your Subconscious

You know when you have succeeded in affirmation by the way you feel. If you remain worried or anxious, if you are wondering how, when, and where or through what source your answer will come, you are meddling. This indicates you do not really trust the wisdom and power of your subconscious. Avoid nagging yourself all day long, or even from time to time. When you think of your desire, lightness of touch is important. Remind yourself that Infinite Intelligence is taking care of it in Divine Order far better than you can through constant worry and effort.

For example, if you say, "I need $10,000 by the fifteenth of next month," or "The judge must make a decision for me by the first of the month or else I will lose my home, my business," and so on, that's a sign of fear, anxiety, and tension. What will that do? Bring blocks, delays, impediments, and difficulties into your life. Always go to the Source. Remember, in peace and in confidence shall be your strength. When you are anxious, tense, and worried, you do not fully believe in the power of your subconscious mind, so it cannot bring about prosperity, or peace of mind, or health, or anything. Go back to the Source. Go to a place of absolute rest in your mind and say to yourself—or rather, reiterate these truths:

> It is done unto me as I believe. All things are ready if the mind be so, which means, all I have to do is ready my mind to receive the benediction, the guidance, the wealth, the answer, the solution, the way out. Divine Light shines in me and through me. The peace of the Everlasting fills my soul. In quiet and confidence shall be my strength.

Reiterate these truths. That will quiet your mind and give you peace. And when the mind is at peace, it gets the answer. For in quietness and in confidence shall be your strength. Infinite Intelligence knows the answer, so learn to let go and relax. Do not give power to the externals or conditions. Give power and allegiance to the Infinite, the presence and power within you.

In swim class you learn that you can float on the water, which will support you if you remain quiet, still, and at peace. But if you get nervous, tense, fearful, you will sink. When you are seeking wealth, prosperity, success, a spiritual healing, or anything, feel that you are resting in the arms of the All Powerful, and realize the Golden River of life, love, truth, and beauty is flowing through you now, transforming your whole being into the pattern of harmony, love, peace, and abundance. Feel yourself swimming in the great ocean of life. That sense of oneness will restore you.

The following meditation will bring many wonderful things into your life. Calm your mind and repeat the following affirmation, accepting it in full faith:

> These truths are sinking into my subconscious mind. I picture them going from my conscious to my subconscious like seeds I am depositing in the soil. I know that I am old-fashioned and create my own destiny. My faith is in the Infinite Being, which created all things and is my fortune. I have an abiding faith in all things good. I live in the joyous expectancy of the best, and only the best comes to me. I know the harvest I will reap in the future, because all my thoughts are Divine Thoughts. Divine Power drives my thoughts of good. My thoughts are the seeds of goodness, truth, beauty, and abundance. I now place my thoughts of love, peace, joy, success, abundance, security, and goodwill in the garden of my mind. This is the Divine Garden. The glory and beauty of the Almighty will be expressed in my life, and I know my garden will yield an abundant harvest. From this moment forward I express life, love, and truth. I am radiantly happy and prosperous in all my ways, and the Living Spirit multiplies my good exceedingly.

To prosper means to succeed, to thrive, and to turn out well. In other words, when you are prospering, you are expanding, growing spiritually, mentally, financially, socially, and intellectually. Never be envious or jealous of another person's wealth, promotion, diamonds, or jewels, for that would impoverish you. That would attract lack and limitation to you.

Rejoice in their success and their prosperity and their wealth and wish for them greater riches, for what you wish for others you are wishing for yourself. What you think about the other person, you are creating in your own mind and experience and also your pocketbook. This is why you rejoice in the success and prosperity that millions of others have. In order to truly prosper, it is necessary that you become a channel through which the Life Principle flows freely, harmoniously, joyously, and lovingly.

I suggest that you establish a definite method of working and thinking—that you practice it regularly and systematically every day.

One young man who consulted me had experienced a poverty complex for many years. He had received no answers to his prayers. He had prayed for prosperity, but the fear of poverty continuously weighed on his mind. Naturally, he attracted more lack and limitation than prosperity. The subconscious mind accepts the dominant of two ideas. Change your mind from belief in poverty and begin to believe in the Divine Abundance all around you.

After talking with me, he began to realize that his thought image of wealth produces wealth; that every thought is creative unless it is neutralized by a counterthought of greater intensity. Furthermore, he realized that his thought and belief about poverty was greater than his belief in the infinite riches all around him. Consequently, he changed his thoughts and kept them changed. I wrote out a prosperity affirmation for him, as follows. It will benefit you:

> I know there is only One Source, the Life Principle, the Living Spirit, from which all things flow. It created the universe and all things therein contained. I am a focal point of the Divine Presence. My mind is open and receptive. I am a free-flowing channel for harmony, beauty, guidance, wealth, and the riches

of the Infinite. I know that wealth, health, and success are released from within and appear in the without. I am now in harmony with the infinite riches within and without, and I know these thoughts are sinking into my subconscious mind and will be reflected on the screen of space. I wish for everyone all the blessings of life. I am open and receptive to the Divine Riches, spiritual, mental, and material; and they flow to me in avalanches of abundance.

This young man focused his thoughts on Divine Abundance rather than on poverty. He made it a special point never to deny what he affirmed. Many people pray for wealth and deny it an hour later. They say, "I can't afford this. I can't make ends meet." They are making a mockery of their prayer. They are like people who constantly talk themselves out of potentially lucrative and fulfilling job opportunities. When the perfect position presents itself, they think of all sorts of excuses for not pursuing it: "I'm really not qualified for that position," "My commute time would be four hours a day!" "I would have to sacrifice time with my partner and children." "My current job isn't all *that* bad." Their mind is divided against itself—desiring the position on one hand and rejecting it on the other. Until the mind is unified, they're unlikely to get the job, assuming they even apply for it.

Well, now, this is the way millions of people "pursue" what they desire. Even in the New Thought movement, practitioners send dozens of conflicting messages to their subconscious mind in a half an hour or an hour. The subconscious is so confused and perplexed it doesn't know what to do, so it does nothing. The result is frustration. *Frustration* comes from the word "*frustrare*"—to deceive, to work for nothing. You don't plant a seed in the ground and then dig it up, so don't contradict what you have affirmed.

This young man focused his thoughts on Divine Abundance rather than poverty, and he stopped saying, "I can't afford . . ." or "I can't buy that piano or that car." Never use the word "can't." Can't is the only devil in the universe. When you say or think "can't," your subconscious takes you literally and blocks all your good.

Now, in a month's time, his whole life was transformed. He meditated on his affirmation morning and evening for about ten minutes, slowly and quietly, engraving the thoughts in his mind, knowing what he was doing, believing what he was doing, knowing that he was actually writing these truths in his subconscious mind, causing the latter to be activated and to release its hidden treasures.

Although this man had been a salesman for ten years with rather dim prospects for the future, suddenly he was made sales manager at $75,000 a year plus prime benefits. The subconscious has ways you know not of. It is impossible to impress upon your subconscious the idea of wealth and be poor. It is impossible to transfer to your subconscious the idea of success and not succeed; the Infinite can't fail. You were born to triumph. Let your affirmation be: "By day and by night, I am advancing, moving forward, and growing. Divine Abundance gives me richly all things to enjoy."

Chapter Takeaways

+ When money is circulating freely in your life, you are economically healthy, in the same manner as when your blood is circulating freely you are healthy and vibrant.

+ To accumulate money to the exclusion of everything else causes one to become imbalanced, lopsided, and frustrated.

+ As you apply the laws of your subconscious in the right way, you can have all the money you want and still have peace of mind, harmony, wholeness, and serenity.

+ Divine Abundance is the source of your supply of energy, vitality, health, creative ideas, the sun, the air you breathe, the apple you eat, and the money in your pocket.

+ Say every day: "I am born to succeed. I am born to win. The Infinite within me can't fail. Divine Law and Order govern my life. Divine Peace fills my soul. Divine Love saturates my mind. Infinite Intelligence guides me in all ways. Riches flow to me freely, joyously, endlessly, and ceaselessly. I am advancing, moving forward, and growing mentally, spiritually, financially, and in all other ways. I know these truths are sinking into my subconscious mind, and I know and believe they will grow after their kind."

+ Constantly affirm, feel, and believe that Divine Being multiplies your good exceedingly, and you will be enriched every moment of the day spiritually, mentally, intellectually, financially, and socially.

+ As you impress eternal truths upon your subconscious mind, watch wonders begin to happen in your life.

CHAPTER 2

Reprogram Your
Subconscious Mind

◆

Many people suffer the consequences of negative thought patterns
programmed into their minds starting the day they were born. Perhaps
they were told that a certain goal was too lofty or led to believe that
"money is the root of all evil." These beliefs are passed to the
subconscious mind, which then manifests them in the person's
experience. If you are the victim of negative thinking, you need to
reprogram your subconscious mind with new, positive beliefs.

To understand how you can create wealth through the power
of your subconscious mind, examine more carefully how this
phenomenon works.

Imagine being hypnotized. In such a state, your conscious, reasoning mind is suspended and your subconscious is amenable to
suggestion. Suppose the hypnotist suggests to you that you are the
leader of your country. Your subconscious would accept the statement as true. Your subconscious does not reason, choose, or differ-
entiate, as does your conscious mind. You would assume all the
airs of importance and dignity that you believe to be concomitant

---

♦

All the powers of the Infinite are within you.

♦

---

of that position. If you were given a glass of water and told that you were drunk, you would play the role of a drunkard to the best of your ability.

If you told the hypnotist that you were allergic to timothy grass, and he placed a glass of distilled water under your nose, telling you at the same time that it was timothy grass, you would generate all the symptoms of an allergic attack; and the physiological and physical reactions would be the same as if the water were actually timothy grass.

If you were told that you were destitute, your demeanor would immediately change and you would assume the attitude of a humble suppliant soliciting donations from passersby.

In short, you may be made to believe you are anything, such as a statue, dog, soldier, or swimmer; and you will act the part suggested with amazing fidelity to the nature of the suggestion insofar as your knowledge extends to the characteristic of the thing that is suggested.

Also remember that your subconscious mind always accepts the dominant of two ideas. That is, it accepts your conviction without question, whether your premise is true or false. Infinite Intelligence dwells within our subconscious minds, regardless of what we call It: God, Subjective Mind, the Living Spirit, Cosmic Power, Allah, Brahma, Jehovah, Great Spirit, or I Am. The point is: It is there within you. All the powers of the Infinite are within you.

The Living Spirit has no face, form, or figure. It is timeless, spaceless, and eternal. The same Spirit dwells in all of us. The Divine

Kingdom is within you, which means that It is in your thoughts, your feelings, and your imagination. In other words, the invisible part of you is the Living Spirit—the Life Principle in you, boundless love, absolute harmony, infinite intelligence.

Knowing that you can contact this Invisible Power through your thought strips the whole process of prayer from its mystery, superstition, doubt, and wonder. Divine Thought, expressed, became all that is, seen and unseen. The Creator commanded everything into being. Every thought is creative and tends to manifest itself in your life according to the nature of your thought. It stands to reason that when you discover the Creative Power, you discover the All Powerful that lives within you. Through the power of your subconscious mind, you possess this Creative Power.

Overcome Negative Conditioning

From infancy on, most of us have been negatively programmed. Not knowing how to reject or thwart negative suggestions, we unconsciously accepted them. For example, you may have been told repeatedly, "Oh, you can't do that." As a result, you may have developed a self-defeatist attitude. Maybe someone said to you, "You'll never amount to anything." Now you have an inferiority complex. Someone may have said: "You mustn't do that; you'll fail." "You haven't got a chance." "You are all wrong." "It's no use." "It's not what you know but who you know." "The world is going to the dogs." "What's the use?" "Nobody cares." "It's no use trying so hard." "You're getting old; your memory is failing." "Things are getting worse." "Life is an endless grind." "Love is for the birds." "You just can't win." "Pretty soon you'll be bankrupt." "Watch out: you'll get the virus." "You can't trust a soul."

If you accept these negative suggestions, you're allowing your subconscious mind to be programmed in a very negative way. As a result, you are at a high risk of developing a sense of inferiority, inadequacy, fear, anxiety, or illness, if you haven't already.

Unless as an adult you program your subconscious mind constructively, which is a reconditioning therapy, the impressions made on you in the past can result in behavior patterns that cause failure in your personal and social life. Reprogramming your subconscious is a means of releasing you from the mass of negative verbal conditioning that might otherwise distort your life pattern, making the development of productive thinking and belief difficult.

Pick up the paper every day and you can read dozens of items that could sow the seeds of futility, fear, worry, anxiety, and impending doom. If accepted, these thoughts of fear could cause you to lose the will for life. Knowing that you can reject all these negative suggestions by giving your subconscious mind constructive autosuggestions, you counteract all these destructive ideas.

Beware of negative suggestions other people express. You don't have to be influenced by destructive, negative suggestions. All of us have suffered from it in our childhood and in our teens. If you look back, you can easily recall how parents, friends, relatives, teachers, and associates may have influenced your thinking with their negative suggestions. Study the things said to you, and you will discover much of it was in the form of propaganda. The purpose of much of what was said was to control you or instill fear. Negative suggestions are common in nearly every home, school, and workplace.

Establish New Thought Patterns

You have the power to reject negative suggestions and replace negative thought patterns with positive ones. For example, suppose Charles is a sourpuss or has a nasty temper due to being told frequently that he's "no fun" or is a "hothead" or due to frustration from often being told that he does not have the talent necessary to engage in a certain activity. One way he can deal with this is to sit down every night prior to sleep and in the morning and the afternoon and affirm as follows:

> Henceforth, I shall grow more in good humor. I shall have more joy and happiness and inner peace of mind. Every day I am becoming more and more lovable and understanding. I am now becoming the center of cheer, cordiality, and goodwill to all those around me, infecting them with good humor. This happy, joyous, and cheerful mood is now becoming my normal, natural state of mind, and I am grateful.

Charles can write the desired qualities in his subconscious; he can reprogram his mind; he can redirect it; and the nature of the subconscious is compulsive; therefore, he will be compelled to be congenial, cordial, a man of goodwill.

He can take these statements, reiterate them, repeat them, remind himself that he is writing these in his deeper mind, and whatever is impressed on the subconscious mind comes forth as form, function, experience, and event. For out of the heart of the subconscious springs life.

In the same way, you can reprogram your subconscious mind. Every morning of your life, sit steady, quiet, get relaxed, and affirm as follows:

Divine Law and Order govern my life. Divine Right Action reigns supreme. Divine Success is mine. Divine Harmony is mine. Divine Peace fills my soul. Divine Love saturates my whole being. Divine Abundance is mine. Divine Love goes before me today and every day, making straight, joyous, and glorious my way.

Repeat these truths frequently. Gradually, by repetition, faith, and expectancy, they will enter your subconscious mind. And whatever is impressed on the subconscious is compulsive. Therefore, you will be compelled to lead a life of harmony, peace, and love.

Fear Not

Many people live their lives in a constant state of anxiety, fear, and even terror, all of which are counterproductive for the operation of the subconscious mind. Worry and fear are negative thoughts energized by a strong anticipation of those thoughts manifesting in one's life. When you worry or fear, you are implanting negative images into the subconscious, which is very dangerous. Worry and fear often cause health issues.

> *Dr. John Sarno, author of* Healing Back Pain: The Mind-Body Connection, *estimates that nearly 80 percent of his patients suffer from tension myositis syndrome (TMS)—inflammation of muscle tissue caused by emotional or psychological stress. His theory is that the subconscious, in an effort to distract the mind from painful repressed emotions, reduces blood flow to certain parts of the body (which vary from patient to patient), causing diverse physical conditions that the patient can focus on instead. After Dr. Sarno*

teaches the patient how to calm the mind (sometimes with the help
of affirmations), the symptoms (in 80 percent of his patients)
disappear. In addition to back pain, Dr. Sarno links TMS to
immune system conditions (including allergies and asthma),
various coronary diseases (including high blood pressure and heart
palpitations), headaches/migraines, gastrointestinal issues, cancer,
and more.

Fear and worry function in a similar way to negatively impact the ability to build wealth. For example, in the stock market, investors often lose a significant portion of their assets due to loss aversion—a fear of loss during a market downturn that leads the investor to sell shares at the worst possible time. Fear and worry also increase a person's aversion to risk. It may, for example, discourage a person from buying a more expensive house, even though it would be a better long-term investment than a more affordable dwelling. Risk aversion may also discourage someone from starting a new business, accepting a new position at work with greater responsibility, or investing in a brilliant invention or business venture. All you need to do is examine the richest and most successful people in the world, and you can see that a large majority of them are optimists with a large appetite for risk.

Think with Your Heart

"As a person thinks in her heart or subconscious, so is she," so does she act, so does she experience, so does she express. This is Cosmic Law.

I am not talking about thinking in the head. I am talking about thinking in the "heart"—what you truly believe subconsciously.

Whatever is impressed there is expressed. Remember, when you are dealing with your subconscious you are dealing with the power of the Almighty. It's the power that moves the world. It's the power that moves the galaxies in space. It's Almighty. There is nothing to oppose It. Consciousness is Divine Being. Unconditioned consciousness is called Awareness; this is the "I Am," the Living Spirit. Your consciousness is the union of your conscious and subconscious mind. It's the sum total of your acceptances, beliefs, opinions, and convictions. It is the only Divine Being you'll ever know.

Your thoughts and feelings create your destiny. If you *think* "poor" you will always *be* poor. Think "prosperity" and you will prosper. Consciousness is the only Creative Power in your life. And your thought and feeling, your conscious and subconscious, are the creator of all you experience. Whatever your conscious and subconscious mind (your brain and your heart) agree to comes to pass, true or false, good or bad. You are the one who is choosing. You mold and fashion your own destiny. Your faith in the Divine is your fortune. Your faith should be in Divine Goodness in the land of the living, and the guidance of Divine Intelligence, and the beauty and glory of the Infinite. That's where it should be.

A man said to me that he wanted to succeed and advance in life, but he really didn't want to. He had a subconscious pattern of failure. He had a sense of guilt and felt he should be punished. With his conscious mind, yes, he worked very hard. And he said to himself, in his intellect, "I work very hard." But in his deeper mind he was programmed and conditioned to fail. He had a sense of unworthiness and a belief that compelled him to fail. He had a picture of failing in his mind. He felt he should be punished, that he was a sinner.

The law of your subconscious, you see, is compulsive. It is the Prime Mover, Almighty Power, Divine Power. This man learned to reprogram his mind by realizing that he was born to win, born to succeed, born to triumph. For the Infinite power is within him. It knows no failure. It's Almighty. It created all things. Nothing exists to oppose It, challenge It, thwart It, or vitiate It. For It is Almighty. It's the only power.

Furthermore, he learned he was punishing himself. To reverse course, every day, morning, noon, and night, he affirmed the following:

> I am born to win. I am born to succeed in my spiritual life, my relationships with people, my chosen work, and all phases of my life. For the Infinite is within me, and the Infinite cannot fail. It's the power of the Almighty moving through me. It's my strength, It's my power, my wisdom. Success is mine. Harmony is mine. Wealth is mine. Beauty is mine. Divine Love is mine. Abundance is mine.

He repeated these truths. He reflected upon them. He reminded himself driving along the road, before he went in to see a customer. He announced these truths regularly and systematically, and he didn't deny what he affirmed.

Gradually, he became a tremendous success, because he succeeded in transforming his subconscious mind into a positive-energy generator through repetition, affirming his inner strength and wisdom; claiming success, harmony, wealth, and abundance; and recognizing his oneness with Supreme Being. As you do this regularly and systematically, wonders will happen in your life.

Divine Powers Live in You

All Divine Powers are within you, and the laws and the truths of Divine Intelligence are written in your own subjective mind. Every night of your life that same Intelligence governs all the vital organs of your body: your breathing, your circulation, your digestion, your heartbeat, and so on.

That's Divine Presence within you. Divine Presence and Power are within you. The great eternal truths are there. They were inscribed in your heart before you were born. But all of us have been programmed since birth. Millions of people have been programmed with certain fears, false beliefs, taboos, strictures, and superstitions. As Phineas Parkhurst Quimby, a pioneer in the New Thought movement, said in 1847, "Every child is like a little, white tablet. Everybody comes along and scribbles something on it: grandmother, grandfather, clergyman, mother, father, sisters, and brothers."

We receive an avalanche of sights and sounds, beliefs and opinions, fears and doubts. You were born fearless (except, perhaps, the fear of falling). You were born without prejudice or bias. You were born without false concepts of the Life Force. Where did you get them? Someone gave them to you. Someone programmed you, perhaps negatively: Many were told they were sinners in the hands of an angry God.

I was taught when I was young that if a child were indoctrinated with a certain religious belief until he or she was seven that no one could change it. Of course, it can be changed, but it's rather difficult. When young, we are susceptible, we are impressionable and teachable. We are amenable to suggestion. Our early receptiveness can be a positive condition, assuming we have parents and other sources of accurate information and wise guidance. However, if our teachers are themselves misinformed, they become a source of untruths and false beliefs. As children, we don't always have the sense to challenge or reject falsehoods and negativity. As a result, we accept many false beliefs and erroneous concepts regarding Divine Being, life, and the universe.

Where did you get your creed or religious belief? You certainly weren't born with it. Is it true? Is it reasonable, logical? Is it supported by evidence? Pat, for example, believes the cards are stacked against him. Some fortune-teller told him that. But the cards are not stacked against him. That is a lie. Divine Being is all spirit, energy, and matter, which cannot be for or against any individual except as that person thinks. Pat has the power to accept or reject the lie. If he accepts it, it becomes a self-fulfilling prophecy. He will stack the cards against himself. If he rejects it and believes the contrary, that the cards are stacked in his favor, he will be rewarded accordingly.

Each person's subconscious assumptions, beliefs, and convictions dictate and control all of that person's conscious actions. If Pat accepts the fortune-teller's lie, the false belief sparks a quarrel in his mind. He may start to suspect that people are working against him, that misfortune will befall him, that he has been jinxed. If he believes the lie, it becomes his law, a law he created for himself that will govern his thoughts and actions and ultimately define his future.

Exercise Your Freedom to Choose

All of us are here to grow, to learn, to release the imprisoned splendor from within. We are not born with our faculties fully developed. You are here to learn. You are here to sharpen your mental and spiritual tools. Joy is in overcoming. Joy is in mastery. You are not an automaton. You have freedom to choose. You have volition; you have initiative. That's the way you discover your Divinity. There is no other way under the sun. You are not compelled to be good. You are not governed by instinct only. Therefore, you have the opportunity to become anything you want to be.

I hold before you an open door that no person can shut. Think on all things that are true, lovely, noble, and Divine. Think on these things all day long. You can begin to recondition your mind. You can picture yourself doing what you long to do because you go where your vision is. Your vision is what you are looking at, what you are thinking about, what you are focused on. And as you continue to focus your attention on that which is lovely and of good report, your deeper mind will respond, and you will be compelled to move forward in the light. For this Almighty Power will move in your behalf.

Keep on reiterating these truths morning, noon, and night. Finally, these truths will sink into your subconscious. Out of the subconscious will come forth whatever you have impressed upon it. Keep thy heart with all diligence. See to it that nothing but Divine Thought and Divine Ideas enter into your deeper mind. Hear the age-old truth again and again until it forms a conviction in your subconscious mind. Hear the absolute truth: I Am and there is none else. One power, One presence, One cause, and One substance. Choose the good, right action. Radiate love, peace, and goodwill to everyone.

When inscribed in your heart, Divine Thought becomes compulsive, and you will be drawn to good and to right action. Some are automatically guided. They have repeated to themselves over and over again: "Infinite Intelligence guides me. Whatever I do will be right. Right action is mine." Morning, noon, and night they reiterate these truths; because there is a principle of right action, there is a principle of guidance, and they are activating it from a universal or infinite standpoint. Those who claim wealth and abundance will have the touch of Midas; all they touch will turn to gold.

Some people wear a talisman, amulet, or charm, such as a cross, a saint's medal, a Buddha, or other religious symbol to constantly remind them of the All Powerful. But you don't need such objects to remind you of the Divine Power within and around you. The main objective is to incorporate these truths in the soul. Because with your thought you are in communion with Divine Intelligence. And you can communicate with It instantly and realize that this Divine Power will fulfill all your needs. You can remind yourself: "The Living Spirit shall supply all my needs according to Its riches and glory. In quietness and in confidence shall be my strength." Remember, to be effective, these truths must be passed from your head (conscious mind) to your heart (subconscious mind).

You must eat the apple before its nutrients can enter your bloodstream. Likewise, you have to absorb and digest these truths. Repetitions do not gain the ear of the Divine; but what you absorb and digest and incorporate in your soul (heart) does. Therefore, announce these truths to your mind regularly and repeatedly, and gradually you will begin to believe and become convinced there is only One Power. It will become a philosophical absolute in your mind that the "I Am" within you is your Creator. This Divine Force is All Powerful, All Wise, and at your disposal twenty-four hours a day, seven days a week, 365 days a year.

Choose Your Lord and Master

Your lord or master is the dominant idea or belief you hold in your mind—your conviction. Suppose you believe in a God of love. Suppose that belief is enthroned in your mind. It's the commanding presence and power influencing your decisions and actions. You give it all your allegiance, devotion, and loyalty. That is your lord, your master. Then you'll lead a charmed life.

For some people, the dominant idea is that external circumstances define their destiny. Others ignore externals and define their own destiny. One person believes she has Divine Intelligence, Infinite Supply, and Divine Omnipotence on her side and that nothing can stand in her way of success and wealth. Another believes she is destined to poverty due to social injustice, her parents having raised her without the confidence and self-esteem to succeed, and employers who engaged in unfair hiring and promotion practices. Both people are correct, because what they believe shapes their reality, but only the first person's dominant idea is true. Perhaps the person who feels disadvantaged must overcome more challenges on her way to success, but many who came before her and faced similar adversity overcame it, and she is fully capable of doing so as well. The only thing holding her back is the dominant idea that governs her life, not the external conditions she encounters or perceives.

Two boys grow up in the same poor neighborhood in Brazil, both in loving, caring families. They attend the same school and play soccer at the same park with many of the same children from the neighborhood. One believes that the only path to wealth is through competition for resources—by taking from others. He falls in with the wrong crowd, shoplifts from local stores, and breaks into homes when the residents are at work. He is constantly struggling to survive and in trouble with the law, and when he gets older, he becomes involved in more serious crimes. The other boy believes in Infinite Abundance and the notion that wealth can be created. His mother bakes bread every morning, and he rides his bike to the market each day to sell it. Over time, he saves and borrows enough money to travel to the United States. Once there, he rents videos and watches them for hours every day to learn English. He visits food pantries and churches to obtain food and clothing and works two jobs, so he can support himself and send home money to his mother. Through his connections at work, he lands a job selling cable TV and Internet service, and quickly becomes the top salesperson in his region. He is promoted to regional sales manager, earning an annual salary of $100,000 plus commissions.

The key difference between these two boys is the dominant idea in their minds. One boy's dominant idea drives him to a life of crime. The other boy's dominant idea leads him to a successful career. Neither boy is defined by the external circumstances in his life. They create their external circumstances through their thoughts, choices, and actions.

Externals have no power except through your own consciousness. Your consciousness is the union of your conscious and subconscious mind. Your conscious mind chooses.

The subconscious mind reacts according to our habitual thinking and imagery. We reap what we sow. What we impress on our subconscious is expressed. When we feed the computer false data or faulty programming code, then, of course, it gives us the wrong answer. We should feed our subconscious mind life-giving patterns.

Have Total Faith

Your affirmation, which is your mental act, must be accepted as an image in your mind before the power of your subconscious will play upon it and make it productive. You must reach a point of acceptance in your mind, an unqualified and undisputed state of agreement. This contemplation should be accompanied by a feeling of joy and restfulness in foreseeing the certain accomplishment of your desire.

The sound basis for the art and science of true programming of your subconscious is your knowledge and complete confidence that the movement of your conscious mind will gain a definite response from your subconscious mind, which is one with boundless wisdom and Infinite Power. The easiest and most obvious way to formulate an idea is to visualize it—to see it in your mind's eye as vividly as if it were alive. You can see with the naked eye only what already exists in the external world. In a similar way, that which you can visualize in your mind's eye already exists in the invisible realms of your mind. Any picture you have in your mind is the substance of things hoped for and the evidence of things not seen. What you form in your imagination is as real as any part of your body. The idea and the thought are real and will one day appear in your objective world if you are faithful to your mental image.

The process of thinking forms impressions in your mind. These impressions, in turn, become manifested as facts and experiences in your life. The builder visualizes the type of building she wants. She sees it as she desires it to be completed. Her imagery and thought processes become a mold and model from which the building will emerge: a beautiful or an ugly one, a skyscraper or a very low one. Her mental imagery is projected as it is drawn on paper.

Eventually the contractor and her workers gather the essential materials and the building progresses until it stands finished, conforming perfectly to the mental patterns of the architect.

You can use this same visualization technique. Still the wheels of your mind and imagine what you would do if you had all the money you needed to be, do, and have all you desire. Imagine the house in which you're living. Envision what you're doing in terms of career or business. Picture the way you're dressed, the vehicle you're driving. Think about the people you're helping to realize their dreams and all the people whose lives you're filling with joy. Build the image in your mind and populate with as much concrete detail as you can imagine. Realize that a picture is worth a thousand words.

William James, the father of American psychology, stressed the fact that the subconscious mind will bring to pass any picture held in the mind and backed by faith. Act as though I am, and I will be. Act as though you now are what you want to be. Play the role in your mind. Do it again and again and again. Gradually, it will sink into your deeper mind and wonders will happen.

Let us realize now that we are going to go by the King's Highway. We will not turn to the right nor to the left. Your way is the Divine Way, and all Divine Ways are pleasant and peaceful. Place yourself under Divine Guidance. Realize that Divine Intelligence is guiding you now. There is right action in your life, and the Living Spirit goes before you making straight, joyous, and glorious your way. Your highway from now on is the royal road of the ancients. It's the middle path of Buddha. It's the straight and narrow gate of Jesus. It is the road to Mecca. Your highway is the King's Highway, for you rule over all your thoughts, feelings, and

> Act as
> though you
> now are
> what you
> want to be.

emotions. Send the messengers of love. They are Divine Messengers—Divine Love, Peace, Light, and Beauty are going before you today and every day to make straight, beautiful, joyous, and happy your way. Always travel the King's Highway; then you will meet Divine Messengers of Peace and Joy wherever you go. Go by the mountain-top road knowing that with your eyes focused on the Divine, there is no evil on your pathway. While driving a car, riding on a train, bus, or airplane, or traveling on foot, realize the Living Spirit always surrounds you. It is your invisible Divine Armor. You go from point to point freely, joyously, and lovingly. The Spirit of the Lord is upon you making all roads a highway for the Divine Power and Intelligence that reside within you.

Your conviction in the Divine Presence is strong and mighty. Know that the spiritual atmosphere in which you dwell goes before you making straight, beautiful, joyous, happy, and prosperous the way. Realize Divine Love fills your soul; Divine Peace floods your mind. And realize that the Divine Power within you is guiding you now, and Its light illumines your pathway. Know there is a perfect law of supply and demand, and you are instantly in touch with everything you need. You are divinely guided in all your ways. You are giving of your talents in a wonderful way. It is written: I will bring the blind by a way that they knew not. I will lead them on paths they have not known.

Chapter Takeaways

+ To create wealth through the power of your subconscious mind, you must first tune in to what you are telling yourself daily and how this may be blocking your path to wealth and happiness.

+ Many of us have been conditioned negatively when we were young. All of us are susceptible to suggestion when we are young and highly impressionable, and we must take steps to convert these false suggestions to positive thoughts.

+ Every morning, sit steady, quiet, and relaxed, and affirm as follows: "Divine Law and Order govern my life. Divine Right Action reigns supreme. Divine Success is mine. Divine Harmony is mine. Divine Peace fills my soul. Divine Love saturates my whole being. Divine Abundance is mine. Divine Love goes before me today and every day, making straight, joyous, and glorious my way."

+ Your thought and feeling create your destiny. If you think you are poor or you have an aversion to wealth or wealthy people, you will always be poor. Think prosperity, and you will prosper.

+ The subconscious mind reacts according to our habitual thinking and mental imagery. We reap what we sow into the fertile ground of our subconscious minds. What we impress on our subconscious is expressed in our lives.

+ Divine Being supplies all you need according to Its infinite abundance.

+ In quietness and confidence is your strength. Divine Truths must reside in your head *and* be felt in your heart.

+ Feel and act as though you are, you do, and you have that which you desire. Play the role in your mind again and again and again. Gradually, it will sink into your deeper mind, and that which you imagine will manifest in your life.

CHAPTER 3

Imagine Your Way to Riches

◆

While the idle brain is the devil's workshop, imagination is God's
workshop. Desire + Vision + Faith = Desired Outcome. Remember that
whatever you desire, envision, and believe, your subconscious mind will
figure out a way to bring to fruition. The secret formula to growing rich
is a strong desire to be rich coupled with a clear vision of being rich
along with total faith that you are rich or will be so soon.

To fulfill any desire, you must form a mental image of its fulfillment and infuse it with positive emotion—desire, gratitude, eager anticipation, and so on—and truly believe that your
desire will be fulfilled. Merely wanting or asking for something
without complete faith that it will be delivered is not enough.

To properly engage the subconscious, take the following steps:

1. Imagine that which you desire. For example, you may
imagine being a doctor caring for your patients, driving a
fancy new car, writing a screenplay, or receiving a fat check for
an invention you just came up with. Having a crystal clear
image in your mind of what you desire is key.

2. Infuse your desire with a positive emotion, such as eager anticipation (faith) of receiving the object of your imagination. Positive emotion is the energy needed to transfer the image from the conscious mind to the subconscious mind.

3. Think of a word or phrase to represent the feeling of being, doing, or having what you imagine, such as "It is mine" or a simple "Thank you." What is important is that you link the word and phrase in your mind with the mental image and feeling of being, doing, or having what you desire.

4. Enter a relaxed state and repeat the word or phrase associated with the feeling of being, doing, or having what you imagine. Whenever you say the word or phrase, *feel* the fulfillment of your desire; for example, if you desire money, feel wealthy.

Spend at least fifteen minutes at least three times daily in this exercise, reinforcing your belief that you will receive that which you desire. Over time, the positive image will be transferred to your subconscious, and the Creative Power within you will find a way and arrange the resources to bring what you desire to fruition.

Never pray for things. Asking favors is not the same as engaging with the Creative Force. The Divine in you must engage with the Divine Power and Intelligence that flows through all things seen and unseen. To engage the Divine Creative Power in you, you must enter a state of consciousness of *being, doing,* or *having* that which you desire. The career, money, and connections you wish to make are the images, likenesses, or physical forms of the states of consciousness which produce them.

Feast in this mood until you are *full* of the feeling of being, doing, or having what you desire; continue until your desire has passed away and you are at peace. This is the point at which your desire has been fulfilled in your subconscious mind (because you no longer desire what you already have). It is then just a matter of time before the object created in your subconscious mind is manifest in the objective world. It may be instant, or it may take several days, weeks, or months. How your desire is fulfilled and how long it takes are not up to you. Trust the details to your subconscious and to the Divine Power within you, because the method and means are outside the scope of human understanding.

Embrace Your Desires

Desire is a Divine Gift. It is Life seeking to express itself through you, because you are a channel of the Divine. You are here to express your divinity in thought, word, and deed. Your basic desire is to express life, love, truth, and beauty. This must be true, for the Living Spirit is Life, which is the nature of the Divine. The tendency of Life is to express itself. The Limitless One does not desire to express Itself in any form of limitation; therefore, death, misery, poverty, or suffering is not the will or desire of the Living Spirit for anyone.

Life does not seek to express death; this would be absurd. Life is wholeness, unity, and integrity. Life always expresses itself in the Cosmos as harmony, health, peace, order, symmetry, and proportion. The whole universe is a paean of harmony, reflecting the great truth that "order is heaven's first law."

You may say, "Maybe my desire is not the will of the Living Spirit for me." If your desire, idea, or intention is to express a greater measure of life, and if it is in harmony with the universal law of good, which is unity, order, and symmetry, it is what the Living Spirit desires for you. The Boundless One does not wish bondage or restriction of any kind. Fundamentally, humanity is good, for the Divine dwells in all of us. The evil that we do and what we suffer as a result are products of our mental aberrations and subjective fears, phobias, and complexes.

Without desire you would not get out of the way of an approaching car. It is because of desire that farmers plant grain, corn, and all kinds of seeds—the desire to feed themselves, their families, and other people. The desire to procreate and to go forth and multiply causes you to seek a mate and generate your kind. Desire is the stimulus that pushes us onward and upward. Thomas Edison desired to light up the world, and we know of his inventions.

A woman said to me, "I do not desire anything. I have everything. We should not desire things." This is nonsense. She had to admit that she desired a cup of coffee in the morning. We live by desire. Without desire, humanity would die.

Thousands of years ago someone desired to deal with the inclemency of the season and made the first house of stone or trees with a roof to block the rain and snow and a fireplace to keep the residents warm. Fireplaces were inefficient and dangerous and did a poor job of heating homes, so around 1855, Franz San Galli invented the radiator. In the summer, houses were too hot, so in 1902 Willis Carrier invented the first modern air-conditioning system. All these things began with desire. Desire is often referred to as the fountain and the origin of all action.

When you speak to your mother, it is based upon your desire to speak to her. When you kiss your child good night, it is your desire to show your love and bless the child.

Desire is the beginning, and the manifestation is the end. When you are ill, you desire health. When you are confused, you desire peace of mind. A poverty-stricken person desires wealth. Your desire is the voice of your savior. As you look at your desire, you are looking into the eyes of your savior. Your desire, when realized, is your savior—your solution—or your salvation. Failure to realize your desire is the cause of frustration, unhappiness, and illness. To continue to desire something morning, noon, and night over a prolonged period of time, yet failing to achieve the goal or receive the answer brings chaos and confusion into your life.

A desire to be greater than you are comes when you are ready. The acceptance of your desire brings you peace. When you consciously unite with your desire in peace and in understanding, its manifestation will appear.

Engage the Power of Faith

Whatever you assume and build into your feeling will become subjectified within you and become objectified on the screen of space (the world around you). You must sustain the assumption; then invariably you will witness its manifestation. *Faith is the substance of things hoped for, and the evidence of things not seen.*

The faith spoken of is your word, conviction, and inner belief. It will not return to you empty. It is the evidence of things not seen. You do not see an unshakeable, unalterable conviction, but it is your evidence or prophecy of that which is to come to pass. States of consciousness always manifest themselves.

You can command that a certain material possession be delivered, and imagine and feel the reality, naturalness, and the solidity of it in your room now. You can imagine the feeling of possessing it and using it. The unseen will become seen in ways you know not of.

The prime condition is faith. To develop a greater faith, shut out all the arguing, challenging, and questioning of the analytical, conscious mind and place a reliance on the power of the subconscious mind. Leave the world of the five senses and enter the Divine World of Spirit.

As you read this, you may say, "Well, I have had a lifetime ambition which has failed to materialize. What will I do?" Distance yourself from anything and anyone who might cause you to question or doubt the power of your subconscious mind. In other words, turn away from sense evidence; give up your limited concept of yourself; realize that you can be, do, and have your heart's desire by the application of this principle.

You must cleanse your mind of all false beliefs and opinions, for it is the conscious mind that argues with you. When you succeed in entering into a fixed psychological state, knowing by an inner certitude that your ideal is embodied within you, you are engaging the creative power of your imagination. Your desire passes away giving birth to the subjective realization of that desire; that is, the object of your desire now exists in your subconscious mind. You are at peace. In a little while your subconscious, in concert with the Almighty, will give birth to your idea. You have given the command, which is your conviction.

You have found that by remaining faithful to your ideal, knowing and believing that the Almighty Power will bring it forth, your ideal is projected on the screen of space. You now give your demonstration attention and nourish it with positive emotion—eager anticipation, gratitude, and faith—increasing its subjective reality.

You believe in your Deep Self now. You give it complete recognition. You have absolute faith in Its Power. You reject sense evidence, and you contemplate the reality of your desire. You are now falling in love with your desire, and you continue to love it. You find your idea is infused with love; it is invincible. You are at peace. You have issued the command, and it will not return to you empty.

Realize the Creative Power of "I Am"

In certain religious texts, Divine Being is referred to as *I Am*, signifying a self-sufficient, all-encompassing being that transcends time and space. Aristotle referred to this entity as the Unmoved Mover or Prime Mover. When you begin a statement with "I am . . . ," you are engaging the Creative Power within you. In fact, the statement "I am" represents your first creative thought; it is the command that brought you into existence. When you say "I am . . . ," you are issuing a command to your subconscious, so be sure that you issue a positive command. If you say, "I am too poor to afford that," you are telling your subconscious to make you poor. If you think, "I am not talented enough to . . . ," you are telling your subconscious to make sure that you lack that certain talent. If you fear that you will lose money through a certain investment, your subconscious will figure out a way to make that happen.

We are and have what we believe. When you say "I am . . . ," how do you describe yourself or your feelings or situation? Do you say, "I am poor, weak, miserable, a failure," and so on? If you say, "I am sick," you are really saying that the Almighty is not feeling well, which is absurd. You must say, "I am strong, powerful, loving, harmonious, kind, gentle, peaceful, and illumined by the Light."

> We are and
> have what
> we believe.

How you complete the sentence "I am . . ." determines whether you are successful, strong, and prosperous or weak, defeated, and full of misery. The reactions of others toward you are also determined by how you perceive yourself.

When you command your subconscious mind, be sure to stay in the present and to issue the command authoritatively, with full confidence that your subconscious mind will execute the command or fulfill your desire. Do not say, "I will be, maybe and perhaps," because that focuses your mind not on what you desire but on what you lack. You are admitting, "I do not have" or doubting you will receive that which you desire.

Also important is that you nurture a feeling in yourself of having received that which you desire. If you merely claim in the silence, "I am wealthy," these words will not produce wealth. You must *imagine* yourself wealthy and *feel* wealthy. The consciousness of wealth produces wealth. Realize that the Creator owns everything and that the Creator in you has full access to that infinite abundance. Divine Abundance is at your disposal.

When your pleasure and desire are for Divine Law or eternal moral and spiritual truths and when you yearn for the vision and the practice of the understanding of the law of harmony and perfection, you are on the way to health, peace, and abundance. Merge in feeling with the One Who Forever Is; then you will bring forth fruit in due season and will find that plans and opportunities present themselves to you, and your ideas come to fruition. Whatever you undertake and whatever presents itself, you will fulfill and execute; moreover, whatever fire, energy, and enthusiasm you need to bring forth your ideal spring from the heavenly tree and are watered by heavenly love and faith.

Prosperity means to increase our capacity or ability in every direction, so that we make use of ourselves and the Divine Cosmic Power fully. We often connect the word "prosper" with a currency, but we do not get more money until we prosper inwardly by learning how to engage our Divine Creative Power.

Admit No Shortage of Supply

According to the law of prosperity, infinite supply and substance are omnipresent; accept this fact in the same manner you accept the luscious fruit off the trees in the orchard; put up your hand and take the fruit from the trees; similarly, acknowledge infinite abundance and claim from it according to your needs and desires.

There is no shortage of air or sunshine; likewise, there is no shortage of supply. Think of supply in terms of the air you breathe. You can breathe in only the amount of air your lungs can hold. Likewise, with money or other material goods, you receive only the supply equivalent to your capacity to receive—what you can imagine and truly believe is yours to claim.

Suppose you want some water at the seashore. If you take a wineglass to the ocean, you can receive only that measure; some people take a gallon container; others a bucket, but they can never exhaust the ocean; there is enough for all. The Source of all good is the one unchangeable Spirit, which is inexhaustible and omnipresent.

Don't think that your goodness or what you receive depends on your job or career. A job is merely one channel through which your supply may come; other channels exist, and they are unlimited in number. When one door closes, another opens.

If you happen to lose a job or position for any reason, adopt a positive attitude. Instead of bemoaning the loss, rejoice and say inwardly that a new, wonderful position is available and yours to claim; then a new position and a better one will come in an easy manner. Become indifferent to the channel and conscious of the Source of good; daily unite with the Unmoved Mover in right thinking, right feeling, and right action.

Feel the Divine Presence; this is an experience in your own consciousness. It is all very well to theorize about the Divine Presence and to think about It, but also develop the inner realization that comes through communing in silence every morning and night. Meditate on the attributes and qualities of the Deity, and you will feel Divine Presence welling up within you spontaneously. You do not see or smell the wind; you feel the breeze upon your face; likewise, you can feel the warmth and the glow of Divine Presence.

Surrounded by Divine Presence, you experience no shortage of supply, so there is no need for competition. You can become wealthy without having to take from others, so avoid any temptation to play the "zero-sum game." In game theory and economics, a *zero-sum game* is a competitive situation in which players gain only at the expense of one or more other players losing something. Chess, for example, is a zero-sum game; for one player to win, the other must lose.

Many people make the false assumption that prosperity is a zero-sum game. It is not. Don't seek prosperity at someone else's expense. Think in terms of creation, not competition. Wealth can be created "out of thin air" as a product of human ingenuity and can benefit more than just you. Entire industries have sprouted from the minds of clever inventors and entrepreneurs. Just look at the automobile and computer industries. Certainly, the inventors and entrepreneurs who have capitalized on these industries have earned enormous amounts of money by harnessing the time, effort, and expertise of others, but they have also employed and produced incomes for millions of people and raised the standard of living overall. Think also of all the artists and musicians who generate wealth through their artistic creations and performances.

> Think in terms of creation, not competition.

Instead of playing the zero-sum game, focus your efforts on generating wealth for yourself for the purpose of attaining self-fulfillment, building a better world, and helping others. Never pursue wealth for the sake of stockpiling money. Think less in terms of savings and more in terms of cash flow; you want sufficient cash flow to pay for everything necessary to be, do, and have what you dream of, and no more. You can't achieve self-fulfillment or fully enjoy your life without resources—education, technology, transportation, communication, and so on—and all of these cost money. But you don't need a surplus, and if you don't spend the money to achieve your dreams and fulfill your desires, it is wasted.

All you need is your "daily bread," and that doesn't mean just enough to survive; it means having enough each day to achieve everything you want to accomplish and to pursue that which you desire. Each person's daily bread varies according to her ambitions, abilities, and desires.

It has been said that it is easier for a camel to pass through the eye of a needle than for a rich person to enter Heaven. The point of that hyperbole is that if your goal is merely to accumulate wealth, you will never achieve self-fulfillment, enjoy all life has to offer, or accomplish much of anything. You will not help those in need or make the world a better place. Money not used is money squandered. It is like electricity; to power lights or machines, it must flow. Your goal is to have a never-ending supply of money flowing through you, empowering you, and providing the fuel you need to pursue your dreams and do good. In such a state of being, you are one with the Divine. You are living in Heaven on earth.

Forget the Past

If you wish to prosper, forget the past; yesterday is dead. However, you can make it alive today by thinking and dwelling on it. Nothing lives but today's mood or feeling; it is your mood that delivers. It is idle and foolish for people to spend their time and energy dwelling upon how wealthy they were at one time. Frequently they say, "Why can't I deliver *now*?" The reason is that to dwell on the past is death and stagnation. By all means rejoice in your past achievements, but never dwell on what you lacked in the past or compare present circumstances as falling short of a measure from the past.

Infinite supply is instantly available *now*. Regardless of what you had or lost in the past, supply is awaiting your claim and recognition. This supply is omnipresent; it is never conditioned by the ebb and flow of your doubt or apprehension. Accept your good now and walk in the assumption that "It is done."

Knowing that supply is endless, never be envious or jealous of another person. When we are jealous of the wealth and success of others, it holds us back and prevents us from achieving prosperity. It raises the other person and lowers us. The Law has no regard for specific individuals; it gives to all according to their belief. Envy is a waste of energy and a destructive emotional force; worse, it is a sign of a false belief in limitation. Rejoice in the success of others, and you attract success to yourself. Realize that the other person belongs to the unified whole, in which you, too, belong.

Profit in Slow Markets

Sometimes real estate agents and homeowners approach me and say, "Times are very slow; real estate is not moving." Real estate—like anything else—is an idea in Divine Mind; all that the owners have to do is to exchange ideas with others. Buying and selling take place in the realm of Divine Consciousness. If you have something to sell, feel and know that Infinite Spirit has now revealed to you the right person at the right time, and that the sale is already accomplished in the realm of Divine Consciousness. Your feeling or conviction that the transaction has already taken place in your consciousness, the only true medium of exchange, gives you confidence and trust. You wait for just a little while and the answer comes—sometimes when you least expect it.

Always remember that Infinite Wisdom has the *know-how* to accomplish any task you assign it; so if you desire a change and wish to sell your property, some merchandise, or an idea to someone else, this Being knows the perfect answer or solution. If the person who would be blessed and made happy by your idea is in China, then he or she would be brought back, and you would be irresistibly attracted to one another. You may not understand the reasoning behind the solution, but the solution will be presented.

Many people ask, "Can I, or should I, get $500,000 for my property?" The answer is in the question. The Golden Rule is the law of life; all else is commentary. If the tables were reversed, would you be willing to pay $500,000? Are you at ease in your own conscience regarding the price? Is it just and equitable in your eyes? If you honestly can answer "yes" to these questions, the price is right.

In all your transactions, remember the Golden Rule: "Do unto others as you would have others do unto you."

When you have property to sell, do you inwardly feel you are overcharging? Do you feel clever in deceiving the buyer? Do you try to take advantage of the other person by subterfuge or underhanded methods? If you do, you are using the law in reverse. You truly prosper when you use the law righteously. People who rob, steal, and cheat develop a fear and guilt complex that ultimately attracts loss to themselves.

Give Thanks That All Bills Are Now Paid

I have talked with many people over a period of years, and a frequent complaint is, "If you saw all the bills that I have to pay—times are terrible!" Instead of fretting about bills, realize that there are no debts in Heaven.

Bliss, harmony, perfect equilibrium, and joy are the states of consciousness called Heaven. Realize that all bills are now paid;

rejoice that it is so. Mark them paid in your own mind by entering into the joyous, happy state that all bills are paid, and drop off to sleep with the words "Thank you" on your lips, thanking Divine Being for all that you are, all that you have, all that you do, and all things good you desire. Give thanks for the gift already received in consciousness. You give the gift to yourself by an inner awareness, feeling, or conviction. In some way all these bills are paid, leaving a divine surplus. You can now decree that you are one with the Infinite Source of supply and that all your needs are met instantly; then watch the Law work!

Master the Law of Reversed Effort

The book entitled *Suggestion and Autosuggestion* by Charles Baudouin and translated by Eden and Cedar Paul brought to the attention of the world the *Law of Reversed Effort*. In the chapter entitled "Laws of Suggestion," the authors state: "When an idea imposes itself on the mind to such an extent as to give rise to a suggestion, all the conscious efforts which the subject makes in order to counteract this suggestion are not merely without the desired effect, but they actually run counter to the subject's conscious wishes and tend to intensify the suggestion." In other words, whenever we are in a doubtful, confused state of mind, and are saying to ourselves, "I should like to, but I cannot," or "I want money to pay my bills, but it is hopeless," we may wish as hard as we please, but the harder we try, the less able we are to manifest our desire.

When we are in financial difficulty, many noxious suggestions present themselves, such as fear, despair, and a complete lack of faith. We become perplexed and feel lost. The harder we try to think the good idea, the more violent is the assault of the bad idea. *Effort is not the way to obtain the desired results.*

Emile Coué originated the *Law of Reversed Effort*. This is Coué's formula in his own words: "When the will and the imagination are at war, the imagination invariably gains the say." Another way of stating it is this: When our desire conflicts with our imagination or belief, our belief wins. The dominant idea always wins. Effort presupposes the idea of resistance that is to be overcome; thus we have two conflicting ideas or suggestions: 1) "I want wealth or money now"; and 2) "but I cannot get it." The two thoughts neutralize one another and nothing happens. It is like mixing an acid and an alkali; the result is an inert substance.

When we say, "I prayed for abundance and for supply *so hard*," we relate the major error of this type of thinking. The way to success is *effortless* and without any struggle. An effortless way is brought about by some forms of hypnosis. We must be careful to note that immobilization of the attention, if it is to produce its proper effect, must be carried out with no sense of strain; we must be able to maintain it with the minimum of voluntary effort.

The condition is analogous to the experience in which people often find themselves on first waking in the morning; they say to themselves that they could get up if they liked, but almost against their will they continue to snuggle under the blankets. Baudouin explains: "A very simple way of securing this [implanting an idea into the subconscious] is to condense the idea which is to be the object of the suggestion, to sum it up in a brief phrase which can readily be graven on the memory, and to repeat it over and over again like a lullaby."

These authors convey that when we enter the sleepy state, or as they describe it, "the state akin to sleep" (between the waking and sleeping state), effort is reduced to a minimum, and we can focus our attention on our good with ease and without strain. We can induce the sleepy state by suggesting sleep to ourselves.

Here is a practical application of the above teaching: A woman in my class said, "Bills are piling up; I am out of work; I have three children and no money, what will I do?" This is what she did: She relaxed her body in an armchair; entered into the sleepy state, and as Baudouin suggested, she condensed the ideas of her needs into the three words: "It is done." The significance of these words to her meant the realization of all her desires, such as: all bills paid, a new position, a home, a husband, food and clothing for the children, and an ample supply of money.

Note the logic of the accepted request in the condensed phrase, "It is done," repeated over and over again like a lullaby. Each time she silently pronounced, "It is done," a feeling of warmth and peace stole over her, until she reached the point of conviction that the objects of her desire were successfully impressed upon her subconscious mind. Her mind did not wander, because she focused and concentrated on one central idea; she repeated it over and over again until it had the feeling of reality.

When we focus our attention on one simple phrase, we prevent the mind from wandering through the network of associated ideas and thoughts. If the mind wanders, bring it back by continuing to repeat the short phrase that means to you the *realization* of all your dreams. Divine Ways are truly past finding out! If I go to a fountain, and I do not have a container, I cannot gather water; likewise, when I go to the fountain of living waters within me, I must have a container, which is my receptive attitude of mind when I am in a passive, joyous state of expectance and acceptance and the single idea or feeling of gratitude dominates.

Consider the case of a man who was having difficulty selling his property; he was very poor. He reclined in a chair, closed his eyes, and immobilized his attention until he started to feel sleepy. As he became relaxed, he entered that drowsy, sleepy state as suggested; it favors results because effort is reduced. *Affirmation should be effortless effort.* He selected the condensed phrase "Thank you"; he repeated it, as if he was addressing the Supreme Being for having accomplished the sale for him. He did not fall asleep the minute he closed his eyes, but he was alert, alive, and quickened by Divine Presence; he entered the silence with an expectant attitude; he knew that he was going to receive that which he desired.

He silently repeated "Thank you," over and over like a lullaby; he continued to speak these words until he had the feeling that all was accomplished. He fell asleep and in a dream (in the fourth dimensional world) he saw a man who gave him a check, and he said to the man, "Thank you, Father." When he awakened, he knew that the property was sold. In a week's time that man he saw in the dream came to him and bought the property, which consisted of fourteen lots, a well, and a home.

The reason for this fourth dimensional experience was that he continued to repeat the words "Thank you" until he fell into the deep of sleep. In the next dimension—where we go every night as we fall asleep—he saw the desired transaction as a concrete, objective fact. The *now* or the *present* in the fourth dimension is equivalent to *here* in the third dimension. Having seen something fourth-dimensionally, we must experience it in the future, in the third dimensional plane.

Start now. Decree silently night and morning that Divine Being is prospering you in mind, body, and affairs; *feel* the reality of it, and you will never want for anything. Repeat over and over like a lullaby, "Thank you, Divine Spirit," as you prepare for sleep; this means you are thanking your Higher Self for abundance, health, and harmony. Truly Divine Intelligence will make Itself known to you in a vision or will speak to you in a dream.

If you are married, take this wonderful opportunity to agree with your mate on the law of abundance; it is an ever-flowing, omnipresent supply of Divine Goodness, Truth, and Beauty. Let husband and wife agree and unite their ideals and motives in the demonstration of abundance along all lines.

Many of the greatest people in all walks of life have been inspired by their spouses. Married people can see each other as they ought to be. Right feeling and inner knowing can transform defeat into success and poverty into abundance. Together they become a driving power and powerful motive for the demonstration of abundance, achieving their agreement with the Creative Spirit.

Chapter Takeaways

+ Imagination is God's workshop.

+ Whatever you desire, envision, and believe, your subconscious mind will figure out a way to bring to fruition.

+ Take the following four-step process to attract riches:

1. Imagine that which you desire.

2. Infuse your desire with positive emotion, such as eager anticipation or faith.

3. Think of a word or phrase to represent the feeling of being, doing, or having what you imagine.

4. Enter a relaxed state and repeat the word or phrase associated with the feeling of being, doing, or having what you imagine.

✦ Desire and hunger are gifts; treat them as such. Desire is the first step to fulfillment.

✦ Whatever you desire, if you have faith that you will receive it, it will be given to you.

✦ Divine Being refers to itself as *I Am*. When you say "I am," you are acknowledging the Divine in you and using your Creative Power to claim that which you desire to be, have, or do.

✦ Admit no shortage of supply, and never envy what others are or have. There is always more than enough to go around. Wealth can be created. Claiming what you desire does not necessarily leave less for others.

✦ Live in today without regret or blame regarding the past or fear about future events that can occur only if you dwell on them.

✦ Be friendly with money. Never allow a thought that money is evil or is the root of all evil. Money is only good or bad as we decide to use it.

CHAPTER 4

Follow a Pattern for Richer Living

◆

Harnessing the power of the subconscious mind to grow rich requires
practice. It works best when you develop a consistent pattern of
thinking and acting prosperous. If you believe one day that wealth is
yours to claim and start hoarding money the next in anticipation of
financial setbacks, you send your subconscious mind mixed signals,
showing that you don't really believe in Divine Abundance.

You were born to win and to triumph over all obstacles in life.
Divinity dwells in you and walks and talks within you. It is
the Life Principle within you. You are a channel of the Divine, and
you are here to reproduce all the qualities, attributes, potencies,
and aspects of the Divine on the screen of space. That is how important and wonderful you are!

Whatever the Creative Force starts, It finishes—whether it be a
star, a cosmos, or a tree. In order to win and triumph in the game
of life, join with the Cosmic Power within you, and as you align
yourself in thought and feeling with this Infinite Power, you will
find the Cosmic Power moving on your behalf and enabling you to
achieve victory and the triumphant life.

How a New Mental Picture of Himself Paid Rich Dividends

"I have been with my firm for ten years and have not received a promotion or a raise in salary. There must be something wrong with me," a man, we will call John, complained bitterly during his first consultation with me. While talking with him, I discovered that he had a subconscious pattern of failure guiding his affairs.

John was in the habit of disparaging himself constantly, saying to himself, "I am no good, I am always passed over, I'm losing my job, there is a jinx following me." He was full of self-condemnation and self-criticism. I explained to him that these were two of the most destructive mental poisons he could generate, and that they would rob him of vitality, enthusiasm, energy, and good judgment, ultimately leaving him a physical and mental wreck. Moreover, I elaborated on his negative statements by pointing out that such statements as "I am no good, I am always passed over," were commands to his subconscious mind, which takes him literally, setting up blocks, delays, lack, limitation, and impediments of all kinds in his life. The subconscious is like the soil, which takes all manner of seeds, both good and bad, and supplies nourishment for their development.

John asked me, "Is this why I am passed over and ignored at our regular business conferences?" My answer was "Yes," because he had formed a mental picture of rejection and expected to be slighted and ignored. He was blocking his own good.

This is how John extricated himself from the patterns of self-rejection, failure, and frustration. I suggested to him that he forget about his past and begin to contemplate the future he desires.

He asked, "How can I forget the snubs, hurts, and rebuffs? It is pretty hard." It can be done, but as I explained to him, he had to come to a clear-cut decision to drop the past and, with positive determination, to contemplate success, victory, achievement, and promotion. Your subconscious knows when you mean what you say and will automatically remind you when, due to habit, you are prone to demean yourself, and you will immediately reverse the thought and affirm the good here and now.

He began to perceive the fallacy, as well as the foolishness, of carrying a mental load of disappointment and failures of the past into the future. It is like carrying a heavy iron bar on your shoulders all day long, thereby bringing about exhaustion and fatigue. Whenever a thought of self-criticism or self-condemnation came to his mind, he faithfully reversed it by affirming, "Success is mine, harmony is mine, and promotion is mine." After a while, the negative pattern was replaced by a constructive habit of thinking.

I gave him the following simple technique to impress positive images upon his subconscious mind. John was to begin to practice the art of picturing his wife congratulating him on his promotion while happily and enthusiastically embracing him. He made this mental picture very vivid and real by immobilizing his attention, relaxing his body, and focusing the lens of his mind on his wife. He would mentally converse with her as follows: "Honey, I received a terrific promotion today, the boss complimented me, and I will receive $10,000 a year more in salary! Isn't it wonderful?" He then imagined her response and heard the tone of her voice, saw her smile and gestures. All were real in his mind. Gradually, this mental movie moved by a sort of osmotic pressure from his conscious to his subconscious mind. Several weeks later, John came in to see me and said, "I had to let you know. They have made me district manager! That mental movie did the trick!"

John, having learned how his mind worked, began to realize that his habitual pattern of thinking, plus his mental movie, were penetrating the layers of his subconscious mind and that the latter was being activated to attract all that he needed to bring his cherished desires to pass.

When you believe and live in the joyous expectancy of the best, you will receive the good you seek. John firmly believed that he would receive honor, recognition, promotion, and a salary increase. According to his belief, it was done unto him.

John is a new man today and a happy one. He is buoyant and bubbling with enthusiasm. There is a light in his eye and a new emotional tone in his voice which indicates self-confidence and poise.

How a Mental Picture Produced a Million Dollars

I had a conversation at a hotel in Palm Springs with a man from San Pedro who told me that at forty, his life was one of disappointment, failure, depression, and disillusionment. He had attended a lecture on "The Miracle of the Mind," given in San Pedro by the late Dr. Harry Gaze, world traveler and lecturer.

He said that after hearing that lecture he began to believe in himself and his inner powers. He had always wanted to own and operate a movie theater, but he had consistently failed at everything and had no money. He began with this affirmation: "I know I can succeed, and I will own and operate a theater."

He told me that today he is worth $5 million and owns two theaters. He achieved success over supposedly insurmountable odds. His subconscious mind knew that he was sincere and that he meant to succeed. It knows your inner motivation and your real conviction.

This man's magic formula for success was the mental picture he carried and to which he remained faithful, and his subconscious mind revealed to him everything necessary for the fulfillment of his dream.

How an Actress Triumphed Over Failure

A young actress came to see me, complaining bitterly about stage fright and panic during auditions and screen tests. She had failed, she said, to make the grade three times; she prolonged her doleful complaints into a lengthy lamentation.

I discovered quickly that her real trouble was that she had a mental picture of panic before the camera and was dooming herself to failure.

I taught this young actress the workings of her conscious and subconscious mind, and she began to realize that as she gave attention to constructive thoughts, she would automatically bring into her experience the benefits accruing from the thoughts dwelt upon. She devised a plan of her own for straight-line thinking, knowing that there is a law of mind which responds to what you decree yourself to be, provided, of course, you believe what you claim to be true about yourself. For example, the more frequently you affirm to yourself, "I am afraid," the more fear you will generate. On the other hand, the more frequently you affirm, "I am full of faith and confidence," the more confidence and self-assurance you will develop.

I suggested she type thought-lifters on a card as follows:

I am full of peace, poise, balance, and equilibrium.

I fear no evil for Cosmic Power surrounds and permeates me.

I am always serene, calm, relaxed, and at ease.

I am full of faith and confidence in the only power there is—Cosmic Power.

I am born to win, succeed, and triumph.

I am successful in all my undertakings.

I am a marvelous actress and am immensely successful.

I am loving, harmonious, and peaceful and feel my oneness with the Divine.

She carried this index card with her. On trains, airplanes, and at frequent intervals during the day, she focused her mind on these truths. After three or four days, she committed them to memory. As she reiterated these truths, they sank down into her subconscious mind and she discovered that these affirmations containing wonderful spiritual vibrations neutralized the noxious patterns of fear, doubt, and inadequacy in her subconscious mind. She became poised, serene, calm, and full of self-confidence. She had discovered the Cosmic Power for Divine Living.

She practiced the following technique for about five or six minutes morning, afternoon, and night: She relaxed her body, sat quietly in a chair, and began to imagine that she was before the camera—poised, serene, calm, and relaxed. She visualized herself as completely successful and imagined hearing congratulatory comments by the author and by her agent. She dramatized the role, as only a good actress can, and made it very real and vivid. She realized that the Cosmic Power that moves the world also moves through the mental picture in her mind, compelling her to give marvelous renditions.

A few weeks later, her agent got another screen test for her, and she was so enthusiastic and exhilarated with the idea of triumph that she gave a wonderful performance. With success following success, she was well on her way to becoming a great star.

You Are Rich and Successful Because of What You Are Inside

I had an interesting conversation with a man at a popular hotel on the island of Hawaii. He told me a fascinating story of his youth. He was born in London, and when he was very young his mother told him that he had been born into poverty, but that his cousin had been born into opulence and a vast fortune because this is the way God equalizes things. He said later he discovered that what she had meant was that in a former life he had been very wealthy, and now God was getting even with him so that He sent him back to earth born into poverty in order to equalize justice.

> ## "You go where your vision is."

"This," he said, "I looked upon as unmitigated balderdash; furthermore, I realized that the Cosmic Law does not discriminate—that God gives to all according to their beliefs, and that a person may be a multimillionaire possessing millions of English pounds sterling and be very illumined and spiritual at the same time. Some of the financially poor people, on the other hand, were most malevolent, selfish, envious, and covetous."

During his youth this man sold papers in London and washed windows; he went to school at night and worked his way through college; he is now one of the top surgeons in England. His motto in life is: "You go where your vision is." His vision was to become a surgeon, and his subconscious mind responded according to the mental image held in his conscious mind.

His cousin's father had been a multimillionaire and had given his son everything possible: private tutors, special educational trips to Europe, and he had sent him to Oxford University for five years. He provided his son with servants, automobiles, and all expenses. The cousin turned out to be a failure! He had been overindulged and had no confidence or self-reliance. He had no incentives, no obstacles to overcome, and no hurdles to rise above. He became an alcoholic and a rank failure in the art of living.

Which one was rich and which one was poor? The surgeon has overcome his obstacles. He said to me that he is thankful that he came up the hard way.

The Chance of a Lifetime
Is Always with You

Recently, a man said to me, "I had no chance in life. I was born into a poor family, and we never had enough to eat. I saw other boys in school whose fathers had lovely homes, private swimming pools, automobiles, and all the money they needed. Life is so unfair!"

I explained to him that often the hardship of poverty can be the impetus to push you to the highest pinnacle of success. A beautiful home, a swimming pool, riches, prestige, success, a luxury car—all are ideas in the mind of man, which is one with the Infinite Mind of Divine Intelligence.

I explained to this man that the thinking of many people is wholly illogical, irrational, and most unscientific. For example, they say that Helen Keller's birth was an injustice, since she was deprived of her senses of sight and hearing in infancy. But she began to use the riches of the mind, and her blue eyes were enabled to "see," probably better than most people, the color of all the pageantry in opera; her deaf ears in a similar manner could "hear" the crescendos, diminuendos, and the full volume of orchestral music. She was perfectly aware of the clear notes of the lyric soprano, and she could grasp the humor of the play.

Helen Keller brought tremendous good into the world. Through meditation and prayer, she awakened the inner eye and uplifted the minds and hearts of the deaf and the blind everywhere. She contributed faith, confidence, joy, and a tremendous spiritual uplift to thousands of shut-ins and others in the world. Indeed, she accomplished much more than many people who have perfect sight and hearing. She was not unfortunate or discriminated against by birth—there is no such thing as underprivileged or overprivileged.

The man was deeply moved by the story of Helen Keller, and I wrote for him the Cosmic plan for success, which he was to affirm fifteen minutes, three times a day, the following:

> I am in my true place in life, doing what I love to do, and am divinely happy. I have a lovely home, a kind and wonderful wife, and a new and up-to-date car. I am giving of my talents to the world in a wonderful way, and Divine Intelligence is revealing to me better ways in which I can serve humanity. I definitely and positively accept the fact that a new and wonderful opportunity is opening up for me. I know I am divinely guided in all ways to my highest expression. I believe and accept abundance and security. I believe marvelous and wonderful opportunities are opening up for me now. I believe I am being prospered beyond my fondest dreams.

He had these affirmations typed on a card, which he always carried with him, and he repeated these truths regularly and systematically for fifteen minutes, three times a day. When fear or anxiety came to his mind, he would pull out the card and reiterate these truths, knowing that the negative thoughts are always obliterated and dissipated by the higher constructive thoughts.

He realized that ideas are conveyed to the subconscious by repetition, belief, and expectancy, and the miracle-working power of his subconscious mind went to work on the impressions made upon it, as its nature is to respond according to habitual thinking.

Three months later, all the things he meditated on came to pass. He is now married and has a lovely home, he has his own business, which his wife bought for him, and he is doing what he loves to do and is divinely happy. He has become a member of the town council and is contributing his time, effort, and expertise to a variety of community service organizations. He had the chance of a lifetime—and so have you!

How a Salesman Helped Himself to Promotion

A pharmaceutical salesman had not received a promotion in eight years; yet other coworkers apparently less qualified had been advanced to higher echelons of the business. His trouble was that he had a rejection complex.

My advice to him was to be nice to himself and to like himself more, because the Self is Divine. I explained to him that he was the house of Divine Being and that he should have a healthy, reverent, wholesome respect for the Divinity within him which created him, gave him life, and equipped him with all the powers of the Living Spirit. This would enable him to transcend all obstacles, to rise to affluence and perfect expression, and to acquire the capacity to lead a full and happy life.

This salesman quickly realized that he could use the same mental energy to think constructive thoughts as destructive ones. He decided to stop thinking of reasons why he could not succeed, and he began to think of reasons why he could become a success. He practiced using the following mental and spiritual formula:

> From this moment forward, I place a new value on myself. I am conscious of my true worth. I am going to stop rejecting myself

and will never demean myself again. Whenever the thought of self-criticism comes to me, I will immediately affirm, "I exalt the Creator in the midst of me." I respect and honor the Self of me which is Divine. I maintain a healthy, wholesome, reverent respect for the Infinite Power within me which is All-Wise and All-Knowing; It is the Ever-Living One, and the Self-Renewing Presence and Power. By day and by night, I am advancing, moving forward, and growing, spiritually, mentally, and financially.

This salesman set aside a certain period three times a day and identified himself with these truths, thereby gradually saturating his mind with poise, balance, and equilibrium, plus a sense of his true values. As a result, after about two months, he became regional sales manager. He wrote to me later, "I am on the way up, thanks to you."

In addition to the above mental and spiritual exercise, and in order to enable him to perceive the true sense of his own worth and importance in the scheme of life as a human being endowed with unique and extraordinary talents and abilities not yet released but dormant within him, I recommended that he practice the age-old *mirror treatment*. This is how he practiced it in his own words:

> Every morning after shaving, I looked into the mirror and said to myself boldly, feelingly, and knowingly, "Tom, you are absolutely outstanding, you are a tremendous success, you are full of faith and confidence, and you are immensely wealthy. You are loving, harmonious, and inspired."
>
> I am one with the Almighty, and one with the Almighty is a majority. I am continuing this practice every morning. I am amazed at the many wonderful changes which have taken place

**in my business, finances, circle of friends, and in my home life.
It has been two months since you gave me these two techniques
of prayer and I have been promoted to regional sales manager.**

This salesman identified himself with the truths he affirmed,
and he established a new image of himself, thereby saturating
his mind with poise, balance, equilibrium, prosperity, and self-
confidence. He believed implicitly in the response of his subconscious mind to his conscious mind activity, thereby discovering the
majestic psychological truth that all things are possible when you
believe.

How an Office Manager Shifted His Perspective

During an interview, an office manager told me that all the men
and women in his office felt that he was too bossy, too critical, and
too gloomy; his office experienced constant turnover, and the general manager had complained about the number of resignations.

I explained to him that overexerting authority usually is a sign of
insecurity; the person is trying to make himself feel self-reliant. A
person can possess a quiet, orderly mind and never order others
around in an arrogant manner, and yet be completely self-reliant;
in contrast, noisy, loud-mouthed persons lack sincerity and inner
balance.

At my suggestion, he began to praise some of the employees for
work well done, and he found that he would usually receive a corresponding friendly response, for by praising them he was building
up their confidence in themselves. He ceased his constant criticism

and carping attitude, which marred the harmony of the office, and he also ceased his self-deprecation, which was the root cause of his trouble.

To eradicate gloom, he began to practice deep breathing in conjunction with a specific affirmation. Breathing in, he affirmed in his mind "I am" and breathing out he thought "cheerful." Through practice he was able to hold his breath a longer time between inhalation and exhalation. He practiced this deep breathing fifty times and a hundred times until he experienced a deep subconscious response. Now he says he gets best results by thinking "I am cheerful" while breathing in and repeating it while breathing out. He has proved the physiological value and sensation of well-being which routinely follows the drawing of deep breaths to aid in the process of impressing constructive ideas upon the subconscious mind.

In addition, he practiced the following mental and spiritual prescription several times daily by affirming as follows:

> From this moment forward, I cease all self-recrimination. I know nothing is perfect in this universe, and I realize that all my employees and associates cannot possibly be perfect in all ways. I rejoice in their confidence, faith, cooperation, and commitment to work well done. I constantly identify with each of my associates' positive qualities.
>
> I am always confident in doing what I know well, and I gain confidence daily in other directions. I know that self-assurance and self-reliance are habits, and I can develop the wonderful habit of self-reliance just the same way as I recently gave up smoking. I supplant timidity with assurance, faith, and confidence in an Almighty Power which responds to my

habitual thinking. I speak kindly to all my employees. I salute the Divinity within them, and I reiterate constantly, "I can do all things through the Divine Power which strengthens me." When thoughts of self-criticism come to me, I supplant them immediately with this truth: "I exalt the Creator in the midst of me."

This office manager made it a practice to affirm these truths about six times slowly, quietly, and lovingly three times a day, knowing what he was doing and why he was doing it. He was building a new, constructive habit which displaced the old. At the end of six weeks, he was a transformed man, full of serenity and inner self-reliance. He was promoted to vice president of the corporation with an income to match.

Chapter Takeaways

+ You were born to win and triumph over all obstacles through Divine Power.

+ Don't talk yourself into failure, as many people do. Think yourself successful, believe it to be true, and success will follow.

+ You become what you contemplate. Cease all self-condemnation, self-criticism, and fear or uncertainty about the future. Contemplate achievement, victory, triumph, and success.

+ When you are tempted to demean yourself, immediately reverse the thought and affirm your good here and now.

+ Ideas are conveyed to the subconscious by repetition, belief, and expectancy. Think only positive, productive thoughts.

+ Believe in yourself and your inner powers. Affirm boldly: "I know I can succeed; I will accomplish what I want to achieve; I will be what I want to be; and I know my Deeper Mind will respond to my honest decision and conviction."

+ If suffering from stage fright, visualize yourself as successful and imagine a loved one congratulating you on your wonderful poise and presentation.

+ You are rich because of what you are inside, regardless of your social or financial status or your education. It is done unto you as you believe.

+ A wonderful formula for success is to affirm with feeling: "Divine Intelligence reveals to me better ways I can serve humanity."

+ Become conscious of your true worth. Realize now that you are a special and unique focal point for the expression of Divine Being.

+ If you feel inferior or lack self-reliance, impress upon your subconscious your oneness with Divine Being by habitually thinking: "I honor and exalt the Divine surrounding me and permeating all that exists. I maintain a wholesome, reverent, and worshipful veneration for the Divinity within me." This attitude builds self-confidence and self-assurance.

+ Praise builds self-confidence among employees and associates. Praise each one for the work well done and realize that no one is perfect in this world. This attitude will banish any bossy and aggressive language or behaviors, which are indicative of insecurity and self-deprecation.

CHAPTER 5

Achieve Success in Your Career

◆

Financial success is often linked to career success. Unfortunately, many
people have a negative attitude about what they do for a living. As a
result, they become stuck in dead-end jobs, doing work they don't enjoy
with people they don't like. They often blame their circumstances on
bad luck or the economy, when what's really at the root of their problem
is a defeatist attitude. If you are dissatisfied or unhappy with your "lot in
life," don't blame fate, external circumstances, or a Higher Power for it;
instead, change your attitude and thinking. This chapter explains how.

For most people, getting rich requires some degree of career
success. We all want to be productive members of society
while doing what we love to do and earning enough money to
have and do what we desire.

Unfortunately, many people struggle in their work life. Some
never land a desirable position. Others enjoy their work but are
frustrated and disappointed with their position or their pay. Some
love what they do but "can't stand the people"—their supervisors,
coworkers, customers, or clients.

This chapter presents a four-step formula for success in your career, along with additional guidance on how to optimize your job and career satisfaction and the compensation you receive in exchange for your time, energy, and expertise.

The Four Steps to Career Success

Many people mistakenly believe that career success relies primarily or solely on external factors; for example, they may say, "It's not what you know, but who you know that counts," or they attribute someone else's success to luck or good fortune—"being in the right place at the right time." These people often fail to give credit to others because they secretly envy them or do not want to admit to shortcomings in themselves that are hindering their own success.

The truth is that career success has more to do with internal than external factors and that everyone has the capacity to achieve his or her desired level of career success.

I have helped many people who struggled in their work lives to achieve rich, fulfilling, and enjoyable careers, and I have distilled the required process into the following four steps to career success:

1. **Embody the personal qualities required for success.**

2. **Discover what you love to do, then do it.**

3. **Specialize in a branch of your field and know more about it than anyone else.**

4. **Be generous, offering your work as a blessing to the world.**

Let's examine these steps in greater detail.

Step 1: Embody the personal qualities required for success. Career dissatisfaction can often be traced to shortcomings in personal qualities, attitudes, or values. Remember, your subjective belief and feeling control your objective life. The images within are reflected on the screen without. If it were possible, for example, to take a photograph of your subconscious beliefs or impressions, they would correspond exactly with your reality. This is true in all aspects of one's life.

The first step toward improving one's position is to improve one's inner self. Strive to become the embodiment of the following divine qualities:

+ Love

+ Joy

+ Peace

+ Patience despite troubles

+ Gentleness

+ Goodness

+ Faith

+ Humility

+ Temperance

When you enthrone these qualities in your mind, you soon become the embodiment of Divine Expression. Who you are and what you do make no difference. Until you are a channel or medium through which these eternal melodies of the Divine are played, you will not begin to bring to fruition your desired career success and personal fulfillment. Your experiences, events, circumstances, and conditions invariably reflect your attitude, values, and virtues.

Peace, harmony, integrity, security, and happiness come from our Deep Self. Meditating on these qualities builds these treasures of Heaven in our subconscious, enriching all facets of our lives.

Step 2: Discover what you love to do, then do it, because enjoying your work generates the energy and passion necessary to achieve success.

For instance, if you are a psychiatrist, it is not adequate for you to get a diploma and hang it on the wall; you must keep up with the times; attend conventions; learn about the mind and how it works. As a successful psychiatrist, you visit clinics and read the latest scientific articles. In other words, you are informed in the most advanced methods of alleviating mental suffering and dysfunction. Successful psychiatrists and doctors must have the interest of their patients at heart.

If you do not know the career or field you should pursue, ask for guidance. Command the Infinite Intelligence within you: "Reveal to me my hidden talents, and guide me to my true place in life." Say this quietly, positively, and lovingly to your Deep Self. As you say this with faith and confidence, the answer will come as a feeling, a hunch, a tendency in a certain direction, or an opportunity. It will come clearly. Ask the effortless way, and the answer comes. Divine Intelligence speaks in peace, not in confusion.

Step 3: Specialize in a branch of your field and know more about it than anyone else. After choosing a specialty, give all your time and attention to it. Become sufficiently enthusiastic and try to know all there is available about this field. If possible, learn more about it than anyone else knows. Become ardently interested in this work, and desire to serve the world. There is a great contrast in this attitude of mind in comparison to that of the person who only wants to make a living or "just get by." "Getting by" is not true success. Your motive must be greater, nobler, and more altruistic; you must want to serve others—as you give, you will receive.

Step 4: Be generous, offering your work as a blessing to the world. Your desire must not be selfish; it must benefit humanity. The circle or complete circuit must be formed. In other words, your idea must go forth with the purpose of blessing or serving the world. It will then come back to you, pressed down, shaken together, and running over. If it is to benefit you exclusively, the circle or complete circuit is not formed.

Some people may say, "But, Mr. James made a fortune selling fraudulent oil stock." One may seem to succeed for a while, but the money this person obtained by fraud usually takes wings and flies away. The injury we give to the other, we give to ourselves. The other is you. *Love your neighbor as yourself.* Your neighbor is yourself.

When we steal from another, we steal from ourselves, because we are in a mood of lack and limitation, which may manifest itself in our body, home life, and affairs.

Whenever someone accumulates a fortune fraudulently, he or she is not successful; success isn't possible without peace of mind. What good is this accumulated money if you cannot sleep nights, are sick, or have a guilt complex?

I knew a man in London who told me of his exploits. He had been a professional pickpocket and had amassed a large amount of money. He had a summer home in France and lived in a royal fashion in England. His story was that he was in constant dread of being arrested by Scotland Yard; he had many inner disorders, which were undoubtedly caused by his constant fear and deep-seated guilt. He knew he had done wrong; this deep sense of guilt attracted all kinds of trouble to him. He served a prison sentence; after that he completely reformed. He went to work and became an honest, law-abiding citizen. He found what he loved to do; then he was happy.

The Law of Reversed Effort Revisited

Success should come without the need for a great amount of conscious effort or energy. The effort should feel effortless. The challenging part is in learning how to pass conscious desires to the subconscious mind and overcome any and all negativity.

French-Swiss psychoanalyst Charles Baudouin presented a unique method for realizing a desire: "A very simple way of securing this is to condense the idea, which is to be the object of the suggestion, to sum it up in a brief phrase, which can readily be graven on the memory, and to repeat it over and over again like a lullaby."

Take the following steps:

1. Relax your entire body; get into a sleepy state; feel sleepy.

2. Focus your attention on your mental image of success.

3. Repeat the word "success" over and over like a lullaby, until you feel yourself to be a great success.

4. Continue to repeat the word "success" until you doze off.

As you repeat the word "success" deeply and lovingly, you induce the mood of success; your mood is creative; then you drop off to sleep feeling successful. This idea of success is impressed upon your subconscious mind, which gives you the ideas, qualities, friends, money, and power that will act on your behalf. The subconscious mind will create circumstances and conditions in harmony with your subconscious belief.

> ## Our thought is creative.

Never underestimate the underlying power of the creative forces of the human spirit. This is the energy that drives all steps in any plan of success. Our thought is creative. Thought fused with feeling becomes a subjective belief, impressed upon the subconscious mind, which brings the subjective belief into objective reality.

Knowledge of a Mighty Power within you, which can bring to pass all your desires, gives you confidence and a sense of peace. Whatever your field of expertise may be, learn the laws of life. "Know thyself" and the way of the spirit. When you know how to apply the laws of life and the way of the spirit, and are giving a service to yourself and to others, you are on the sure path to true success. If you are involved in Divine Business, or any part of It, Divine Presence, by Its very nature, is for you, so nothing can stand in your way. When you accept this understanding, no power in heaven or on earth can withhold success from you.

Believe in Yourself

An engineer said to me once, "I have failed to accomplish three assignments given to me. I failed miserably." This man began to see that he feared and expected failure. He completely changed his mental attitude. He admitted, "I have had faith in failure. From this moment forward, my faith will be in success." His motto became, "Anything I can conceive and believe possible, I can achieve." Inscribe this quotation in your heart.

Yes, anything you can conceive, you can achieve. This engineer began to realize there was an Almighty Power within him, which he could tap; he began to find the answers—the power and wisdom to accomplish things he previously believed to be hopeless. Now he has faith in success; he expects success. Faith is contagious; everyone working under him, likewise, became imbued with the idea of success.

Let me tell you of a young woman, Mary, who visited me after listening to one of my lectures in New York City. She asked the age-old question: "How can I learn to believe in myself?"

We are dealing with all levels of consciousness, and I met the young woman at her level. I responded with a simple question: "What do you need most at this moment?"

I know some of you reading this book will say, "I want Divine Knowledge, Truth, Wisdom, and Understanding." This, of course, is the highest desire, but her answer was, "A sewing machine!"

The next step was to teach her how she could get the sewing machine. I explained that a machine is a Divine Idea.

This is what she did: She sat down on her sofa one evening, became quiet, relaxed, stilled her mind, and imagined a sewing machine in front of her. She felt the reality and solidity of the machine with her imaginary hands; in her imagination she was using it. She went to sleep thanking the Source of all things seen and unseen.

The sequel of her prayer is interesting. A woman who lived in the same apartment building knocked on Mary's door and asked her if she wanted a sewing machine; the woman was giving it away, since she was leaving for her honeymoon. Mary accepted!

Mary said, "This thing works!" She had proved it to herself. Now she wanted a piece of tapestry for the wall; that came, too, as a result of her affirmation. "In the same way I can become a great dancer, also," mused Mary. We know that in order to assume something, we must build the nature and the character of the thing assumed into our consciousness. We build it into our feeling. Mary's senses denied she was the great dancer; however, she knew how to use the law, which gave her faith and confidence; her understanding of the law enabled her to demonstrate her desires. It was no longer a blind faith born of ignorance, but a faith born of Divine Understanding. She knew that any idea felt as true becomes subjectified, and the subconscious mind brings it to pass in its own way. She also knew that this law responded to negative ideas as well as positive thoughts. She learned that the subconscious mind was like a mirror: whatever image or idea she held before it would be reflected in the objective world.

We know that negative ideas will not hurt anyone unless they are energized by a charge of fear, anxiety, anger, or some other negative emotion; nor will positive thoughts do much good, except as we feel them to be true in our own heart.

Mary walked the earth knowing and believing she was a great dancer; thus she created a mental atmosphere around her, which attracted to her all the qualities and attributes necessary for the fulfillment of her dreams. The money, friends, teachers, introductions, and all other things essential for her development and progress were drawn to her. In time she was employed in a dancing academy and became a teacher of teachers.

Chapter Takeaways

+ The way you think or feel about the world is not controlled by your situation or circumstances (your "lot in life"). It is just the opposite—the way you think or feel about the world controls your experiences and the situation and circumstances in which you live.

+ Success should come without the need for a great amount of conscious effort or energy. The challenging part is in learning how to pass conscious desires to the subconscious mind and overcome any and all negativity.

+ Believe in yourself and your ability to achieve the career success you desire. You are Divine and, through your subconscious mind, you have all the energy, matter, and Divine Intelligence of the cosmos at your disposal.

CHAPTER 6

Take Control of Your Life

❖

Most people let other people and outside forces control their lives.
Instead of living their lives proactively, they live reactively at best,
accepting what they falsely believe is their lot in life. In short, they allow
themselves to be pushed around by people, situations, events, and
circumstances. You can take control of your life by shifting focus from
the ever-changing world around you to the eternal Divine Truth and
Power that reside within you.

I constantly receive letters from all over the country and from many foreign countries, and I find that most of the writers personally experience great vacillations of fate and fortune.

Many write and say something along these lines: "I get along fine for several months, in both health and finances, and then suddenly I find myself in the hospital or I meet with an accident or experience a great financial loss." Others say, "Sometimes I'm happy, joyous, vital, and bubbling over with enthusiasm, and suddenly an acute wave of depression seizes me. I can't understand it."

I have just finished interviewing a business executive who, some months ago, had reached what he termed the pinnacle of success and then, to use his own words, "the roof fell in" on him. He had lost his home, his wife had left him, and he lost a considerable sum of money on the stock market.

He asked me, "Why did I rise so high and fall so suddenly? What am I doing wrong? How can I control these ups and downs?"

How This Busy Executive Learned to Control His Life

This executive wanted to get away from these swings of fortune and health and lead a balanced life. I explained to him that he could steer his life in the same manner as he steers his car to work every morning: The green lights say to go ahead; you can take your foot off the brake and step on the accelerator. You stop at the red lights and, following the rules of the road, you arrive at your destination in Divine Order.

I gave him the following spiritual formula with instructions to affirm these truths in the morning before getting into his car, in the afternoon after lunch, and at night prior to sleep:

> I know that I can steer my thoughts and imagery. I am in control, and I can order my thoughts to give attention to what I desire. I know Divine Power resides within me which I am now resurrecting and which responds to my mental call upon It. My mind is Divine Mind, and I am always reflecting Divine Wisdom and Divine Intelligence. My brain symbolizes my capacity to think wisely and spiritually. I am always poised, balanced, serene, and calm. Divine Ideas govern my mind and are in complete control; I no longer am subject to violent swings of mood, health, and wealth. My thoughts and words are always

constructive and creative. When I pray, my words are full of life, love, and feeling; this makes my affirmations, thoughts, and words creative. Divine Intelligence operates through me and reveals to me what I need to know, and I am at peace.

The executive made a habit of reciting this affirmation regularly, systematically, and with conviction, and as he continued to do so, gradually he reconditioned his mind to harmony, health, serenity, and poise. He no longer suffers from those changes in fortune of which he spoke, and he is leading a poised, balanced, and creative life.

How a Teacher Conquered Her Frustration

A teacher opened an interview with me with these remarks: "I'm in a rut. I feel frustrated; I have failed in love. I'm sick in mind and body. I am full of guilt, and I feel intellectually incompetent. Henry David Thoreau was right when he said that the mass of men lead lives of quiet desperation!"

This young lady was very intelligent, well-read, and intellectually competent, but she was demeaning herself and was full of self-condemnation and self-criticism, all of which are deadly mental poisons that rob you of vitality, enthusiasm, and energy, and leave you a physical and mental wreck.

I explained to her that all of us have our ups and downs, our depressions, griefs, and illnesses, until we decide to control our lives and do our own constructive thinking. Otherwise, all of us would be subject to the mass mind which believes in sickness, accident, misfortune, and tragedies. Furthermore, we feel that we are subject to conditions and environments and that we are victims of our early training, indoctrination, and heredity.

Our state of mind, and our beliefs, convictions, and conditioning determine our future. I explained to her that her present condition was due simply to the habitual force and authority of many thousands of thoughts, images, and feelings which she had consciously and unconsciously acquired and repeated through many years.

"Furthermore," I added, "you have said that you have traveled all over the world, but you have not traveled anywhere within yourself. You are like the elevator operator who says, 'I go up and down all day long, but I don't get any place in life.' You are repeating the same old patterns of thinking and idle wishing—the same routine procedures, plus constant mental agitation, turmoil, and grievances against your superiors, your pupils, and the school board."

She decided to make a definite change, to get out of the old routine, and to begin to experience the beauties, the satisfactions, and the glories of life. She affirmed the following truths several times daily, knowing that what she accepted consciously would find its way to her subconscious mind, and that by repetition she could recondition her mind to the success, happiness, and joy of life which she deserved to experience. She took the following spiritual medicine several times daily, affirming as follows:

> I am going to travel mentally and spiritually within myself and discover the treasure house of eternity within my depths. I am definitely and positively going to break old routines. I am going to go to work by a different route every morning and will come home by a different way. I will no longer think according to the headlines of the newspapers or listen to gossip and negative

thoughts about lack, limitation, disease, war, and crime. I know that everything I do and experience in life is due to my thinking—conscious or unconscious. I realize that if I do not think for myself, the mass mind impinges on my subconscious mind and does my thinking for me, which is mostly negative and destructive.

A revolution is now taking place in my mind, and I know that my life is transformed by the renewal of my mind. I immediately cease railing and mentally fighting conditions, as I know that this attitude magnifies my troubles. I now affirm and rejoice that I am an expression of the Divine and that my Creator needs me where I am; otherwise, I would not be here. Divine Being is active in my life, brings me harmony and serenity.

Repeating this affirmation several times daily worked wonders in the life of this college teacher. As she turned on the green light of constructive, confident thinking and became certain in the knowledge that all mental seeds deposited in the subconscious grow after their kind, love came into her life; she married the president of the college! She has received promotion in her profession, and she has had inner spiritual experiences, discovering that she had a great talent for painting, which has brought her endless joy. She is now releasing the imprisoned splendor within. Truly, affirmations positively impact your life.

The Cosmic Law of Action and Reaction

A pharmacist confided to me, "I am down in the depths! How can I go up the ladder? Thieves stole thousands of dollars of merchandise and money from my store, and my insurance covers only part of the loss. I have lost a small fortune in the stock market. How do you expect me to think constructive thoughts about that?"

"Well," I replied, "you can decide to think whatever you choose about anything. What you have lost has nothing to do with the way you decide to think about it. It is not what life does to you, it's the way you react to it."

I pointed out to this pharmacist that neither the thieves nor the stock market had the power to steal from him his nights and days, his health, the sun, the moon, or the stars.

I also pointed out to him, "You are rich mentally and spiritually. You have a loving, kind, and understanding wife and two wonderful boys in college. No one can steal from you your knowledge of pharmacy, pharmaceutical chemistry, or your business acumen and sagacity—all these are riches of the mind.

"The thieves have not taken away from you your knowledge of the law of your subconscious mind or the way of the Infinite Spirit within you. It is foolish for you to dwell on the negatives. Chant the beauty of the good! It is now time for you to stir up the Divine Gift within you and to go forward in the light. Get in league with Divine Presence and Power which will restore to you manifold all the riches of life.

"Now," I said, "you know that you cannot gain or lose anything except through your mind; therefore, you will not admit the loss, but you will identify mentally and emotionally with the seventy thousand dollars you have lost, and whatever you mentally claim and feel to be true, your subconscious will honor, validate, and manifest for you. This is the law of action and reaction which is cosmic and universal."

Accordingly, he affirmed as follows:

I am constantly on my guard against negative thinking, and I cast it out of my mind whenever it enters. I have faith in the Infinite Power and Presence that always works for good. My faith is in the goodness and guidance of the Living Spirit. I open my mind and heart to the influx of the Living Spirit, and I discover an ever-increasing sense of power, wisdom, and understanding.

I am mentally and emotionally identified with the $70,000, and I know that I cannot lose anything unless I accept the loss—which I positively, definitely, and absolutely refuse to accept. I know the way my subconscious works. It always magnifies what I deposit in it; therefore, the money comes back to me pressed down, shaken together, and running over.

I know that I will no longer experience the ups and downs of life, but that I will lead a dynamic, creative, balanced, and purposeful life. I know that affirmation is the contemplation of Divine Truths from the highest standpoint. I know that the thoughts and ideas I habitually dwell upon become dominant in my mind, and they rule, govern, and control all my experiences. My family, my store, and all my investments are watched over by the overshadowing Divine Presence, and the whole armor of the Almighty surrounds me, enfolds me, and enwraps me. I bear a charmed life. I know that eternal vigilance is the price of peace, harmony, success, and prosperity. With my eyes focused on the Almighty, no evil can block my way.

The pharmacist made a habit of reiterating and affirming these eternal verities. After some weeks had passed, his broker called him and gleefully informed him that he had recuperated all his losses due to a rebound on the stock market. Furthermore, he received a wonderful offer for a piece of land he had held for ten years; he sold it for $60,000, his original investment in the land being $5,000.

He has discovered the wonderful workings of his mind and realizes he does not have to suffer from the ups and downs of life.

Rise Above the Mass Mind

The mass mind simply means the mind operating in billions of people in this world. All thought enters into one universal mind, and it does not take much stretch of the imagination to realize the kind of imagery, feelings, beliefs, superstitions, and ugly, negative thoughts are impressed on that universal mind.

It is also true that millions throughout the world are pouring into the mass mind thoughts of love, faith, confidence, joy, goodwill, and success, plus feelings of triumph, accomplishment, and victory over problems and an emanation of peace and goodwill to all. However, they are still in the vast minority, and the dominant feature of the mass mind is one of negativity.

The mass mind believes in accidents, sickness, misfortune, wars, crimes, disasters, and catastrophes of all kinds. The mass mind is rampant with fear, and the children of fear are hate, ill will, resentment, hostility, anger, and suffering.

It is, therefore, very simple for anyone who wants to think at all to realize that she will be subject to trials and tribulations of all kinds until she learns to harness the power of the mind scientifically— and to keep up her armor of protection. All of us are subject to the influence of the mass mind, the spell of negativity, the sway and power of propaganda, and the opinions of others. And as long as we refuse to think intentionally, we shall experience the violent swings of fortune and misfortune, suffering and well-being, wealth and poverty. If we refuse to think for ourselves from the standpoint of eternal principles and truths, we will be only one of the mass and will inevitably experience the extremes of life.

Take complete control of your mind through constructive thinking and visioning, and then you will neutralize the negative suggestion of the mass mind which is forever attacking the minds of all of us. You can rise above the negative mass mind by identifying with the principles of harmony, health, wealth, peace, joy, wholeness, and perfection. Make a habit of doing so, and by the law of attraction you will draw into your life and experience Divine Qualities and Attributes.

The following is an excellent affirmation which will enable you to rise above the mass mind and establish an immunity to the false beliefs and fears of the masses:

> Divine Presence flows through me as harmony, health, wealth, peace, joy, wholeness, beauty, and perfection. The Living Spirit thinks, speaks, and acts through me. I am divinely led in all my ways. Divine Right Action governs me. Divine Law and Order govern my entire life. I am always surrounded by the sacred circle of Divine Eternal Love, and healing light surrounds and enfolds me. Whenever my thoughts wander away in fear, doubt, or worry, I know it is the mass mind thinking in me. Immediately, I boldly affirm, "My thoughts are Divine Thoughts, and Divine Power is with my thoughts of good."

Continue to identify with and to meditate on the above affirmation, and you will rise above the discord, confusion, and extremes and tragedies of life. You will no longer experience the ups and downs, but rather, you will enjoy a constructive, vital, and active life full of creativity and lucrative opportunities.

Some months ago, a woman from North Carolina wrote me, saying that the world is going to the dogs, that our morals are at a low ebb, that corruption is rampant, and that teenage violence, crime, and scandal are the news of the day. Then she added, "We may be annihilated by an atomic bomb any day. How do we tune in to the Divine in the midst of all this degeneracy, pornography, and the cesspool of iniquity in which we find ourselves?"

I admitted that what she said was true, but that we must separate ourselves from the masses. She must have the ability and capacity to rise above the world negation and to lead a full and happy life right where she is. I pointed out to her that all she had to do was to look around and she would find thousands of people who are happy, vital, joyous, and free, leading constructive lives, and contributing to humanity in countless ways.

We have witnessed the extremes of the Victorian period with all its sexual taboos and restrictions, and these repressions caused people to move to the opposite extreme that we are experiencing today in the immorality and lewdness prevalent in various parts of the world.

The ancient Hebrew wisdom says: "Change eternal is at the root of all things." You must find an anchor within you to tie to and make a Divine adjustment. Tune in to the Infinite Power within you and let Its presence guide, direct, and govern you in all your ways. You can enthrone Divine Wisdom in your conscious mind by claiming that It anoints your intellect and is a lamp unto your feet and a light on your path. Following is an affirmation I gave to the troubled woman in North Carolina:

I realize that I cannot change the world, but I know I can change myself. The world is an aggregation of individuals, and I know that people who are ruled by the mass mind, propaganda, and five-sense world are subject to the tragedies, sorrows, accidents, illnesses, and failures in life until they learn to control their minds with Divine Ideas which heal, bless, inspire, elevate, and dignify their souls. I realize that the mass of people are under the sway of the mass mind, full of errors, false beliefs, and negation of all kinds.

From this moment forward, I no longer fight conditions or situations, and I cease rebelling at news of subversives, immorality, and corruption in high places. I write constructive letters to congressmen, senators, movie producers, and newspapers, and I pray for right action, beauty, harmony, and peace for all people everywhere. I am in tune with the Infinite, and Divine Law and Order govern my life. I am divinely guided and inspired. Divine Love fills my soul, and waves of light, love, truth, and beauty go forth as a mighty wave of spiritual vibration which tends to lift all people up.

This young lady recently phoned me and said, "Your letter was the greatest eye-opener I have ever read. I'm on 'cloud nine'! Now I know that change must start with me and what I think. Being in tune with the Infinite, I am in tune with Divinity in the hearts of all men and women in the world!"

Chapter Takeaways

+ Steer your thoughts, images, emotions, and reactions to life as you would steer your car in the right direction.

+ Order your thoughts to give attention to the desires, goals, and objectives in your life. Only you can control your thoughts, which define your destiny.

+ When you repeat your affirmations, infuse your words with life, love, anticipation, gratitude, and other positive emotions.

+ Until you take control of your thoughts and emotions, you are subject to vacillations of fortune and misfortune and to the negativity of the mass mind.

+ Many people travel all over the world but go nowhere within themselves. Travel within, mentally and spiritually, and you will discover in your depths the riches of Heaven.

+ Everything you do and experience in life is a product of your conscious and subconscious thinking. Think good and good follows.

+ You can decide to think whatever you choose about anything. What you have lost or suffered has nothing to do with the way you decide to think about it.

+ You cannot lose anything unless you admit the loss in your mind.

+ The mass mind is dominated by negative thought and emotion— it is full of the fears, doubts, superstitions, hates, jealousies, greed, and lust of billions of people.

+ You can rise triumphantly over the negativity of the mass mind by enthroning in your mind ideas which heal, bless, inspire, elevate, and dignify your soul.

+ Tune in with the Infinite and feel and know that Infinite Intelligence governs, controls, and directs your life, and you will lead a balanced and creative life free from the great swings of fate.

+ You can lift yourself above all the servitude and bondage of the mass mind by exalting the Divine in your midst and realizing that Divine Love fills your soul and Divine Wisdom anoints your intellect.

CHAPTER 7

Unleash Infinite Power to Benefit Every Aspect of Your Life

◆

> Life and all that life offers is meant to flow through us—it is meant to be used and shared. When we distance ourselves from others and greedily hold on to our wealth, talents, and experiences, we cease to grow and develop as human beings. Even worse, we pass a belief of limitation to our subjective minds, which act on that belief. To allow riches to flow into our lives, we need to let them flow out, as well, by using those riches to benefit ourselves and others.

During my lecture tours, I once addressed a group of people in the mountains of Colorado. In the course of a conversation later at a luncheon, my host said that most people worry too much and thus deprive themselves of a full and happy life.

He told me of an elderly man who had lived in one of the cabins in the mountains nearby. The neighbors felt sorry for him because he always seemed to be tired, depressed, worried, and lonesome. He wore tattered clothes and owned a run-down car built in the 1970s. He seemed to have nothing to live for, and he apparently had no relatives or friends. Occasionally he went to the grocery store and invariably asked for stale bread and the most inexpensive food, and he usually paid for it in frugally doled out pennies and nickels.

When he did not appear for a couple of weeks, the neighbors went to his cabin and found that he had died. The sheriff searched the old cabin for names of relatives or a clue to his real identity. To everyone's amazement, they found that the poor old man had more than $100,000 in bundles of $25. He evidently had made much money in his earlier years and had never invested it or deposited it in banks.

He had acquired considerable money, but he had failed to use it to lead the rich life or to spend it for an altruistic purpose. Further, he failed to invest it wisely for interest and dividends. My host said that it was fear that had dominated the old man. He had worried lest people might learn of his money and steal it from him. He had been a very negative thinker, yet he had had a fortune within and without to share in the good life. He could have had much enjoyment and happiness.

You Have a Fortune to Share

The treasure house of infinity is within you. You have the key to unlock the storehouse of all kinds of treasures. The key is your thought, which will bring you far more wealth of every description than that lonely and fearful old man had—and much more of everything you want!

You have the key to the most wonderful and marvelous power in the world—the power of the Infinite within you. Seek first the knowledge and awareness of this inner Divine Presence and Power, and all things you want shall be added unto you.

Remember, your powers are the powers of the Creator, which the average person habitually and through ignorance fails to use. You have a fortune to share by stirring up the gift of the Living Spirit within you. You can share the gifts of love and goodwill with others; you can share a smile and a cheerful greeting; you can give compliments and appreciation to your coworkers and employees; you can share creative ideas and Divine Love with all those around you.

You can see Divine Intelligence and Divine Wisdom in your sons and daughters and call it forth knowingly and feelingly, and what you claim and feel will be resurrected in their lives. You can have a new idea worth a fortune which you can share with the world—perhaps a sonata, an invention, a play, a book, or a creative and expansive idea in your business or profession which will bless you and others.

Remember that the only chance you have is the one you make for yourself. You have the chance of a lifetime! Begin now to mentally tap the infinite reservoir within you, and you will find yourself moving onward and upward.

Rise to the Heights of Your Desires

Some years ago, during a lecture, Mrs. Vera Radcliffe, our church organist in Los Angeles, told the stirring drama of Ignacy Paderewski's trials and tribulations before he became a world-famous pianist. He had been advised by the famous composers and authorities on music in his day that he had no possible future as a pianist and that he should forget about it. The professors at the Warsaw Conservatory, where he went to study, tried their best to discourage his desire. They pointed out that his fingers were not well-formed and that he should try writing music instead.

Paderewski rejected their negative pronouncements and identified himself with his inner powers; he subjectively realized that he had a fortune to share with people throughout the world, namely, the melody of the Divine and the music of the spheres.

He practiced arduously and diligently for hours every day. Pain tortured him in thousands of his concerts. He persevered, however, and his stick-to-itiveness paid fabulous dividends. The inner powers responded to his call and to his effort. He knew that the key to his triumph was his contact with the Divine Power within him.

As time went on, Ignacy Paderewski's musical genius was acknowledged all over the world, and people of all walks of life paid homage to this man who touched and sensed his oneness with the Great Musician within—the Supreme Architect of the universe itself.

Like Paderewski, you have the power to reject completely the negative suggestions of those in authority who tell you that you cannot be what you want to be or have what you desire. Realize, as did Paderewski, that the Divine Presence which gave you the desire and the talent is the same Power that will open the door and reveal the perfect plan for the fulfillment of your dream.

Trust the Divine Power within you, and you will find that this inner presence and power will lift you up, heal you, inspire you, and set you on the high road to happiness, serenity, and the fruition of your ideals.

How to Cope with Seeming Worldly Injustice

During a visit to Hawaii, a junior executive said to me, "There is no justice in the world. Everything is so unfair. Corporations are soulless; they have no heart. I work hard and spend long hours after closing time, but men under me are promoted and I am passed up. It's all so unfair and unjust."

My explanation was the cure for this man's wrath. I acknowledged that there is injustice in the world and that, as Robert Burns said, people's inhumanity to one another makes countless thousands mourn, but that the law of the subconscious mind is impersonal and eminently fair at all times.

Your subconscious mind accepts the impress of your thought and reacts accordingly. It's the set of the sails, and not the gales, that determines the way you go. It is your inner thought, feeling, and imagery—in other words, your mental attitude—operating within you, rather than the winds of negative thoughts and the waves of fear from without, that makes the difference between promotion and success, and between failure and loss. The law is just and mathematically accurate, and your experiences are the exact reproduction of your habitual thinking and imagery.

I briefly explained to the young executive the familiar story of the laborers in the vineyard, where all the workmen received a penny. Even those who came in at the eleventh hour received the same wages as those who worked all day long; also the men who came in at the third hour, the sixth hour, and the ninth hour received the same wages. When they saw that the men who had worked but one hour got the same wages, they were jealous and angry, but the answer they received was this: Did you not agree to work for me for a penny?

> It's the set of the sails, and not the gales, that determines the way you go.

I explained that by focusing his thoughts on injustices at work, he was "selling himself short." His conscious thought was being passed to his subconscious, and by not changing his thinking, he was "agreeing to work for a penny." Instead, he needed to take control of his thoughts and command his subconscious to deliver the status and compensation he desired.

I added, "You are resentful, angry, and full of condemnation and criticism of your employer. These negative suggestions enter your subconscious and have resulted in loss of promotion, financial increase, and prestige."

I gave him the following mental and spiritual formula to practice daily:

I know that the laws of my mind are just and that whatever I impress on my subconscious mind is reproduced mathematically and accurately in my physical world and circumstances. I know that I am using a principle of mind, and a principle is impersonal. I am equal before the laws of mind, which means it is done unto me as I believe. I know that justice means fairness, rightfulness, and impartiality, and I know that my subconscious is impersonal and impartial.

I realize that I have been angry, resentful, and jealous, and that I have also demeaned, criticized, and condemned myself. I have psychically persecuted, assailed, and tortured myself, and

I know that the law is "as within, so without"; therefore, my boss and associates attest to and confirm objectively what I have thought and felt subjectively.

What I accept completely in my mind, I will get in my experience, regardless of conditions, circumstances, or the powers that be. I wish success, prosperity, and promotion for all my associates, and I exude goodwill and blessings to all people everywhere. Promotion is mine; success is mine; right action is mine; wealth is mine. As I affirm these truths, I know they are deposited in my subconscious mind—the creative medium— and wonders are happening in my life.

Every night of my life, prior to sleep, I imagine my wife congratulating me on my wonderful promotion. I feel the reality of all this, mentally and emotionally. My eyes are closed, and I am drowsy, sleepy, and in a passive, receptive state of mind, but I hear her congratulatory words, feel her embrace, and see her gestures. The whole mental movie is vivid and realistic, and I go off to sleep in this mood, knowing that Divine Intelligence delivers as I sleep.

This executive discovered that the law of his mind established justice (conformity to the principles of his mind). Having enthroned right thoughts, right imagery, and right feeling in his conscious mind, his subconscious responded accordingly, leading to improvement in his external circumstances. This is the equity of the mind. The laws of your mind are the same yesterday, today, and forever. At the end of a few months following this affirmation process, this executive was voted president of his corporation and is prospering beyond his fondest dreams.

How a Woman Shared Her Fortune and Got Richer

A few years ago, I had many interesting talks with a Canadian woman. She informed me that she looks upon money and wealth like the air she breathes. She felt as free as the wind. Ever since she was a child, this woman had claimed: "I am rich; I am God's daughter; God gave me richly all things to enjoy." This was her daily affirmation.

She has accumulated millions of dollars and has endowed colleges and universities, establishing scholarships for worthy students and hospitals and nurses' training centers in remote parts of the world. Her joy is in giving wisely, judiciously, and constructively, and she became richer than before.

She said to me one day, "You know, the old aphorism is absolutely true: 'The rich get richer and the poor get poorer.' To those people who live in the consciousness of affluence and abundance, wealth flows by the cosmic law of attraction. Those who expect poverty, privation, and lack of all kinds are living in the consciousness of poverty, and by the law of their own mind they attract more lack, misery, and deprivation of all kinds."

What she said is true to some degree. Admittedly, people born in certain locations or with certain advantages have more resources and opportunities for success. For them, positive thinking may come easier than for those raised in poverty. However, wealth is still a product of a person's thinking and what that person does with the resources and opportunities available. It is the only explanation of how one individual can rise from poverty and riches while others, with a similar background, physical and cognitive abilities, education, and other talents and resources, remain impoverished their entire lives.

Many people who are living in poverty are envious and resentful of the wealth of their neighbors; this mental attitude results in even more lack, limitation, and poverty in their lives. They are, unwittingly, blocking their own good. Yet they have a fortune to share if they would but open their minds to the truth of being and realize that they, too, have the key to unlock the treasure house or gold mine within.

The following illustration shows how anyone has a fortune to share.

His Fortune Was Where He Was, but He Was Blind to It

A friend of mine who lived in northern Alaska once wrote me and said that life was unbearable. He felt that he had made a tragic mistake in going to Alaska to seek his fortune, that his marriage was a complete failure, that prices were exorbitant, and that cheating and overcharging were rampant. When he had gone to court to dissolve his marriage, the judge was crooked, and he got a raw deal. He concluded by saying that there is no justice in this world.

What he said was true enough. All we need do is tune in to the morning news to find stories of crime, corruption, conspiracy, abuse of power, and other injustices—but we must remember that all these are manufactured, and we can separate ourselves from the masses.

You can rise above the mass mind, human cruelties, and greed by aligning yourself with the principle of right action and absolute justice within you. Divine Being is absolute justice, absolute harmony, all bliss, boundless love, fullness of joy, absolute order, indescribable beauty, absolute wisdom, and supreme power. All these are Divine Attributes, Qualities, and Potencies. When you dwell on these qualities and contemplate Divine Truths, you rise above the injustice and the cruelties of the world and you build a conviction to counter all its false beliefs and erroneous concepts.

In other words, you build up a Divine immunity—a sort of spiritual antibody—to the mass mind. While this may not make you fully immune to suffering the consequences of other people's negative thinking and actions, it prevents other people's negative thoughts from taking up residence in your mind and it places you on a path that is less likely to cross the path of those who engage in such thinking and behaviors.

This explanation was a prelude to my direct reply to my friend. I wrote to him, suggesting that he stay where he was and that I suspected he wished to run away from his responsibilities and was merely seeking an escape. I wrote a short affirmation, as follows:

> Where I am, Divine Being is. Divine Being dwells in me and needs me where I am now. This Divine Presence within me is Infinite Intelligence and Wisdom and reveals to me the next step, opening up for me the treasures of life. I give thanks for the answer, which comes to me as an intuitive feeling or an idea which wells up spontaneously from my mind.

He followed my advice and was eventually reconciled with his wife. He bought a camera and took pictures of northern Canada and Alaska, wrote short stories, and amassed what he considered a small fortune. A year passed and for a Christmas present he sent me $2,000, suggesting that I take a vacation in Europe, which I did.

This man had found happiness by tapping the treasure house within, and he discovered that his fortune was right where he was.

How a Professor Discovered a Fortune

Recently I talked with a college professor who was very angry over the fact that his brother, a truck driver, was earning $85,000 while he was earning only about $65,000. He said, "It is all so unfair. We must change the system. I worked hard and toiled for ten years to get my Ph.D., and my brother didn't even graduate high school!"

This professor was brilliant in his field, but he was unaware of the laws of mind and the gross disparities of income I observe daily. I explained that he could rise above the mass mind, the five-sense mind, the mind that thinks from the standpoint of circumstance, conditions, and traditions.

Accordingly, at my suggestion, he began to practice the "mirror treatment" every morning, which consisted of standing before the mirror and affirming: "Wealth is mine. Success is mine. Promotion is mine now." He continued affirming these statements for about five minutes every morning, knowing that these ideas would be recorded on his subconscious mind.

Gradually, he began to feel the way he would feel were all these conditions true, and at the end of one month's time he received an offer from another university at $100,000 a year. Suddenly he discovered a flair for writing, and his manuscript was accepted by a large publishing house, which will bring him a sizable income.

The professor discovered that he was not a victim of "the system" or the scheduled salary scale outlined by the university. His fortune lay in his discovery of the hidden power within himself.

How a Woman's Faith Worked Wonders for Her

A legal secretary complained to me as follows: "I never get the breaks. The boss and the other people in the office are mean and cruel to me. I have been mistreated at home and by my relatives all my life. A jinx must be following me. I'm no good. I should just give up!"

I explained to her that she was mentally cruel to herself, and that her self-flagellation and self-pity must have substantiation and confirmation on the external plane of life. In other words, the attitudes and actions of those around her attested to and conformed with her inner state of mind.

This woman, at my behest, pictured herself being congratulated by her employer for expertise and attention to detail, and she also imagined him announcing an increase in salary for her. Daily, she constantly diffused love and goodwill to everyone she encountered.

Having faithfully sustained her mental image throughout each day for several weeks, she was completely dumbfounded when a colleague not only congratulated her on her work but furthermore asked her to marry him! In a few hours' time, as I finish this chapter, I will have the pleasure of being the officiating clergyman.

She has found the key which unlocked the treasure house.

Chapter Takeaways

+ Your fate and fortune begin with you. Your thought and feeling create your destiny. All Divine Powers, Attributes, and Potencies are locked in your subconscious mind, and you have the key— what you choose to think and feel.

+ Call on the Infinite Intelligence within you for creative ideas, and you will receive them. Ask and you shall receive.

+ Through perseverance, endurance, and determination, you can rise to the heights of your profession or ideal in life. Set your sights high!

+ You have the power to completely reject the negative, limiting statements of others and to trust the Supreme Power within you which never fails.

+ The sails, not the gales, determine your fate and fortune. Position your sails in the right direction. Disregard the inequities and injustices of the world.

+ If you agree with life "for a penny a day," life responds accordingly.

+ Whatever you impress on your subconscious—good or bad—will appear as form, function, experience, and events in your life.

+ Realize that your Creator gave you richly all things to enjoy. Claim these gifts, and riches will flow into your life.

+ The more you give, the more you will receive.

+ Your fortune is right where you are. You can rise above the apparent lack and limitation of the world by mentally and emotionally uniting with the good you desire.

+ If you want to make more money and to enjoy the rich and abundant life, stop comparing yourself with others and being envious of their wealth or success.

+ Faith is the confident expectancy that the mental image you sustain in your mind will become your reality.

CHAPTER 8

Overcome Obstacles through the Secret Power of Self-Mastery

◆

People often make the mistake of looking outside themselves, to the five-sense world, to find solutions to their problems. They blame how they think and feel about the world (and other people) on their situation and circumstances—their external realities. The truth is that all answers and solutions reside within them in the form of Divine Truths. Any and all external obstacles can be resolved through self-mastery—becoming a master of one's own thoughts, ideas, beliefs, and actions.

Even when you are perfectly aligned with the Cosmic Power of Mind, you will encounter difficulties, challenges, and problems. They may seem overwhelming and overpowering, but if you have faith in the Infinite Power, you will affirm boldly the following:

> Be thou gone. I will overcome this challenge through the Infinite Power. This problem is divinely outmatched. I will grapple with it courageously, knowing that all the power,

wisdom, and strength necessary will be given to me. I have unquestioning faith that Divine Intelligence knows the answer, and I am one with It. Divine Intelligence reveals to me the way out, the happy ending. I walk in that assumption and as I do, I know the obstacle will disappear—will be gone out of sight, dissolved in the light of Divine Love. I believe this; I accept it wholeheartedly; it is so.

How to Apply Self-Mastery in Your Life for Richest Blessings

Some time ago I interviewed a woman who had been in the hospital for about two months suffering from bleeding ulcers and what she called a nervous breakdown. The root cause was likely related to domestic and financial stress. She said her husband was suspicious of her; he gave her a low weekly sum to run the house and buy food for two children, and then wondered where all the money went. He would not permit her to go to church because he felt that all religions were just "rackets." She loved to play music, but he wouldn't allow a piano at home.

She complied with his distorted, twisted, morbid ideas, thereby frustrating her own innate desires, talents, and capacities. She deeply resented her husband, and her suppressed rage and frustration brought on her nervous collapse and ulcers. Her husband was playing havoc with her emotions because of his ignorant, selfish, callous opposition to her ideas and values.

I explained to this talented woman that marriage is not a license to browbeat, intimidate, and suppress the aspirations and personality of the other. I pointed out to her that in marriage there must be mutual love, freedom, and respect and that one must cease being timid, dependent, fearful, and subservient. She must become psychologically and spiritually free and seek fulfillment in all facets of her life she desires to do so.

In talking with both the husband and the wife, I suggested that each one cease being a scavenger; that is, dwelling on each other's shortcomings, weaknesses, and foibles, but instead, begin to see the good in each other and the wonderful qualities which they admired in each other when they married. The husband was quick to see that the resentment and suppressed rage of his wife was the cause of her ill health. They arrived at a plan whereby the wife could express herself musically and socially. They also agreed to open a joint checking account based on mutual love, trust, and confidence. Most of all, they agreed to a pattern of affirmation focused on the Living Spirit and Divine Peace, acknowledging its presence in themselves and each other.

Both the husband and wife remained faithful to their agreement and prayer life. They knew that to believe something is to bring it to pass. "Believe" is made up of two words, "be" and "alive." The old English meaning of the word is to "live in the state of being," which means making it real in your life. At the end of about a month, I received a phone call from the wife saying, "I became alive to (believed) these truths which you wrote out for me. They are registered in my heart (subconscious mind)." The husband added, "I am now master over my thoughts, emotions, and reactions, and my wife is master over hers. Self-mastery is a real thing in our lives." They discovered that the Infinite Power for perfect living is always within themselves.

How a Discouraged Young Man Gained Self-Esteem and Recognition

A young man complained to me that he is constantly slighted in social gatherings and is also passed over for promotion in his organization. He added that he frequently entertains in his home, but that he is never invited as a guest to the homes of his associates and others whom he has entertained. He held a deep and violent animus in his heart toward everyone.

While this well-educated young man conferred with me and shared his childhood and home environment, he informed me that he had been brought up by a puritanical New England father. His mother had died at his birth. His father, who was somewhat tyrannical and despotic, frequently said to his son, "You're no good. You will never amount to anything. You are stupid. Why aren't you smart like your brother? I am ashamed of your school record." I discovered that this man hated his father. He grew up with a rejection complex and unconsciously felt unacceptable to people. To use a vernacular expression, he had a psychic boil and was terribly touchy in the field of human relations. This was accompanied by a subjective expectation and fear of being rejected by others, either by rude affront or by what is commonly called "the brush-off."

I pointed out to him that in my estimation he was constantly fearing slights and rejection; furthermore, he was projecting his animosity and resentment of his father onto others. Compulsively he wanted to be disparaged, rejected, or dismissed by someone's manner, attitude, comment, or by what seemed to be a greater interest in others. I explained to him the law of his mind and gave him a very practical plan for overcoming his rejection complex and assuming mastery over his life.

The first step to solving a problem of this type is to realize that no matter what the past experiences may have been, these can be completely eradicated by feeding the subconscious mind with eternal verities and life-giving patterns of thought. Since the subconscious mind is amenable to suggestion and controlled by the conscious mind, all negative patterns, complexes, fears, and inferiorities can be expunged. These are the life-giving patterns:

> I recognize these truths to be true. I am a son of the Living Spirit, which dwells in me and is my real self. From this moment forward I will love the Divine within me. Love means to honor, respect, give allegiance to, and be loyal to the only presence and the only power. From now on I respect the Divinity which shapes my ends. This Divine Presence within me created me, sustains me, and is the Life Principle within me. I love all others as I love myself. My neighbor is the closest thing to me, because the Divine in me is the Divine in him. Every conscious moment of the day I honor, exalt, glorify, and have a healthy and reverent respect for the Divine Presence within me. I know that as I exalt and have a healthy and wholesome respect for the Divine Self within me, I will automatically respect and love the Divine in the other person. Whenever I am prone to criticize or find fault with myself, I will immediately affirm, "I honor, love, and exalt the Divine Presence within me, and I love the Divine in me more and more every day." I know I cannot love and respect others until I first love, honor, respect, and pay loyalty and devotion to my real Self—my Divine Self—in the midst of me, which is mighty to heal. Honoring the Divine within myself, I will honor the dignity and Divine Royalty of all people. I know these truths, when repeated feelingly, knowingly, and believingly, enter my subconscious mind; and I am subconsciously compelled to express these truths, as the

> nature of my subconscious mind is compulsion. Whatever is
> impressed, I am compelled to express. I believe this implicitly.
> It is wonderful!

The second step is to reiterate these truths frequently, three or four times a day, to establish a habit of constructive thinking.

The third step is never to condemn, demean, or demote yourself. The moment a thought comes to your mind such as, "I'm no good," "a jinx is following me," "I'm unwanted," or "I'm nobody," immediately reverse the thought by saying, "I exalt the Divine in the midst of me."

The fourth step is to imagine yourself mingling with your associates in a friendly, amiable, and affable manner. Imagine and hear your superiors congratulating you on a job well done. Imagine you are being welcomed and accepted graciously into the homes of your friends. Above all, believe in your image and in its reality.

The fifth step is to realize and know that whatever you habitually think upon and imagine or fear must come to pass, for that which is impressed on your subconscious mind must be expressed on the screen of space (the "real" world) as experiences, conditions, and events.

This young man diligently followed the above procedure, knowing what he was doing and why he was doing it. Having a knowledge of the way his subconscious mind worked, he gained confidence daily in his technique and application. Gradually he succeeded in cleansing his subconscious of all the early psychic traumas. He is now welcomed into the homes of his associates and has been entertained by the president and vice president of his organization. Since adopting these psychological procedures, he has received two promotions and is now executive vice president of his bank. He knows that application of the Cosmic Power within him brings self-mastery over the past or conditions, experiences, and events. It is done unto you as you believe.

How a Couple Overcame Marital Unhappiness

Recently I received a letter from a woman in Texas:

> **Dear Dr. Murphy:** I read your book *The Cosmic Power Within You*, from which I received great help. I would like your advice on my problem. My husband is constantly criticizing me using abusive, sarcastic, and vitriolic language. The mendacity of my husband makes it impossible for me to believe anything he says. He sleeps in a separate room, and there is no marital intimacy. No matter what kind of community work I do, he finds fault. In the last five years we have had no guests in our home. I am full of antipathy toward my husband. I am afraid I am beginning to hate him. I have left him twice. We have had spiritual counseling, as well as psychological help and legal advice. I can't communicate with him. What shall I do?

My reply was as follows:

> **Dear "Debra":** You can't afford to resent or hate anybody in the world. Such feelings or attitudes are mental poisons

which debilitate the entire mentality and rob you of peace, harmony, health, and good judgment. They corrode your soul and leave you a physical and mental wreck. You are the only thinker in your world, and you are responsible for the way you think about your husband—he is not. My suggestion to you is that you stop trying to communicate with him and surrender him to God completely, lock, stock, and barrel. It is wrong to live a lie. It is better to break up a lie than to live it. There is a time in our experience when, having done everything we can to solve a problem, we should follow the injunction of Paul, "Having done all, I stand"; that is, you stand on the Cosmic Wisdom within you to solve the problem. You have visited psychologists, lawyers, and pastors, obviously in a spirit of goodwill, to bring about a healing; but, apparently, there is no solution in sight. Turn your mind to constructive pursuits and adopt a new attitude toward your husband, such as, "None of these things moves me."

Here is a pattern of affirmation which, when followed by you, will bring results, for the Cosmic Power never fails:

I surrender my husband to the Creator, who made him and sustains him. The Creator reveals to him his true place in life where he is divinely happy and divinely blessed. Cosmic Wisdom reveals to him the perfect plan and shows him the way he should go. Cosmic Power flows through him as love, peace, harmony, joy, and right action. I am divinely guided to do

the right thing and to make the right decision. I know that
what is right action for me is right action for my husband;
also, I know that what blesses one blesses all. Whenever I
think of my husband, and no matter what he says or does, all
I do is to affirm knowingly and feelingly, "I have surrendered
you to the Creator." I am at peace about everything, and I
wish for my husband all the blessings of life.

I recommended that she cultivate a constructive life of her own, expressing her talents and continuing in community projects. I advised her to remain faithful to the specific affirmation, explaining to her that these Divine Thoughts would cleanse her subconscious mind of all resentment and other negative and destructive poison pockets lodged in her deeper mind. This would be done in the same way as clean water drop by drop will, if we persist, cleanse a pail of dirty water so that we will have clean water to drink. You can, of course, turn the hose on a pail of dirty water and get clean water faster. The hose, figuratively speaking, would be a transfusion of Divine Love and Goodwill into the soul, bringing about an immediate cleansing. However, a gradual cleansing process is the usual procedure.

The sequel to the above prayer process is interesting, as the following letter reveals:

Dear Dr. Murphy: I am deeply grateful for your letter, advice, and prayer technique, which I have followed faithfully. When my husband became sarcastic and poured forth expletives and invectives, I blessed him by silently affirming, "I surrender you to the Creator." I became interested in hospital and community work and have made many friends the last six weeks since I started praying. My husband asked for a divorce last week, to which I gladly agreed. We have already made a property settlement which is mutually satisfactory. He is going to Reno for a divorce and plans to marry a woman whom I feel is right for him. I have fallen in love also with a childhood sweetheart of mine, whom I met in my hospital work. We are to be married as soon as I am legally free.

Truly the Living Spirit works in mysterious ways Its wonders to perform. While the marriage ended, more important is the end of her own mental anguish. She freed herself of it, and all parties have found the respectful love and partnership they deserve.

Chapter Takeaways

+ Realize that every problem is divinely outmatched. Meet every challenge with courage and confidence. Command that the mountain (obstacle) be cast into the sea (dissolved, obliterated from sight), and it will be so according to your faith.

+ The quickest and surest way to overcome discouragement is to give of your talents, love, kindness, and consideration wholeheartedly to others. Perform some act of kindness for another, visit a hospital or a sick friend, volunteer in your community, or give others a transfusion of loving kindness.

+ To embody Divine Presence, maintain thoughts of Divine peace, harmony, joy, wholeness, beauty, illumination, love, and goodwill in yourself and others.

✦ Husbands and wives should identify with the good qualities in each other and with the characteristics that initially endeared one to the other. As they see the Divine Presence in each other and exalt that Presence in one another, harmony will prevail, and the marriage will grow more blessed through the years.

✦ Husbands and wives should not try to suppress the personalities of one another. A person whose personality is suppressed becomes frustrated and neurotic. Each should rejoice in the full expression and fulfillment of the other.

✦ Persistence pays great dividends. Remain faithful to your affirmation process in order to maintain and strengthen your faith. According to your belief is it done unto you.

✦ If you feel constantly slighted and rejected, this is usually due to an underlying expectation of being treated this way. To address the problem, focus on the Divine Presence within you; crowd out of your mind anything inconsistent with Divine Presence.

✦ When you have honestly tried every conceivable way to solve a problem, hand it over to the Divine Intelligence that resides within you, and it will reveal the solution.

CHAPTER 9

Engage Your Head, Heart, and Hand

◆

What makes human beings uniquely creative is a combination of
faculties that can be summarized as head, heart, and hand—thought,
feeling, and action. Throughout these writings, I focus mostly on heart
(feeling), specifically desire, faith, gratitude, and so on, which play a
crucial role in impressing positive images upon the subconscious mind.
The focus is on the subconscious, because it is the source of our Divine
Nature, the ground in which we plant the seeds of our desire, and the
driver of thought and action. However, we are most creative and
successful when we engage all three faculties—head, heart, and hand.

Although we are Divine Beings in a sense that all spirit, energy, and matter is Divine, we may consider ourselves to be
part Spirit and part human or physical. Our subconscious mind
(heart) is Spirit—the part of us that is at one with Divine Intelligence, Divine Omnipotence, and Infinite Abundance. Our conscious minds and our physical bodies are human traits, which
enable us to exist and function in this three-dimensional, five-
sense world. These three faculties together enable us to not only
desire and innovate but also, through conscious thought and action,

bring our desires, ideas, and inner talents to fruition. Our conscious minds and our physical senses also enable us to fully enjoy everything life has to offer on this physical plane.

Unfortunately, many people miss out on opportunities by engaging only one or two of these three faculties. For example, they may engage the conscious mind to impress upon the subconscious mind a desire and then, when the subconscious presents the object of that desire (for instance, a lucrative innovation), they fail to act on it. Perhaps the idea was in the form of a mental image of an invention that the person did not transfer as a drawing to paper or invest the time and effort or money to have patented. Or, they may have a talent for music or acting that they did not develop. Some people are presented golden opportunities that they fail to pursue, even when little more is required than a decision to do so—a simple "yes."

In contrast, people who engage all three faculties—who dream big, think creatively and analytically, and act with conviction—pursue their desires with gusto and seemingly cannot be stopped from achieving their goals. They are certain they will excel at whatever they do, overcome any obstacles, and obtain all they desire. These are the movers and shakers of the world, and they are blessed with golden opportunities.

> *With a net worth upward of $86 billion, Bill Gates is one of the wealthiest people in the world. He did not achieve that mark by positive thinking alone or by just transferring a desire from his conscious to his subconscious mind. He and his business partner, Paul Allen, used their heads and hands—conscious thought and action—to design software that revolutionized the computer industry, enabling everybody to use computers to perform practical tasks. Through their efforts and expertise and that of other*

designers and developers, the personal computer has become a virtual necessity in nearly every office, school, and home.

Gates first became captivated by computers and began programming them in 1968, at age thirteen. In 1973, he entered Harvard University as a freshman, where he developed a version of the programming language BASIC. In 1975, Paul Allen, Gates's friend from Lakeside School in Seattle, Washington, who was then a programmer at Honeywell, saw a picture of the first micro-computer, the Altair 8800, on the cover of a copy of Popular Electronics. *Allen bought the magazine and brought it to Harvard to show Gates. Together, they recognized the potential to develop an implementation of BASIC for this new system.*

By the time he reached his junior year, Gates was so absorbed in his dream of building a software company that he left Harvard to devote his energies to fulfilling this dream. He and Allen formed a company, Microsoft, as the vehicle for this endeavor. Guided by a belief that the computer would be a valuable tool on every office desktop and in every home, they began developing software for personal computers. Gates's foresight and his vision for personal computing have been central to the success of Microsoft and the software industry.

Having achieved his major goal, Bill Gates continues to pursue new goals both in the business of creating ever-improving computer programs and in his philanthropic work, having founded with his wife, Melinda, the largest charitable foundation in the world.

By reading this story, you can see how Divine Intelligence orchestrated the process and resources required to enable Allen and Gates to achieve their dream, but without their conscious thought and action, they would never have brought their dream to fruition.

The Head: Leverage the Power of Conscious Thought

Your conscious mind plays a key role in impressing images upon your subconscious mind. Whatever you choose to imagine in your conscious mind and infuse with strong emotion is impressed upon the subconscious mind, which then finds a way and the resources to make real.

Because the conscious mind is analytical and often challenges what is possible, suspending the conscious mind may, at times, be necessary to prevent it from undermining the workings of the subconscious mind. However, the conscious mind (the objective, thinking mind) plays a key role in choosing which desires and opportunities to pursue and in coming up with new ideas and plans to bring them to fruition. As such, it should remain fully engaged in the conscious creative process as soon as the subconscious delivers the gift or opportunity.

The conscious mind has the following four essential functions:

+ **Attention:** The conscious mind chooses what to focus on at any given moment, whether that happens to be current sensory perceptions, information extracted from perceived data (such as the meaning of written or spoken language), or information recalled from memory.

+ **Reasoning/analysis:** As data flows into the brain via the senses, the conscious mind filters, organizes, and tries to make sense of it. Its capacity to filter data is especially important, because the conscious mind guards the door of the subconscious mind to prevent false information and potentially harmful messages from being transferred to the subconscious.

✦ **Decision:** Your conscious mind ultimately decides or chooses. It decides which desires to pursue, which images get passed to the subconscious mind, and when and how to act when opportunities arise.

✦ **Imagination:** Imagination is abstract thinking; for example, the ability to extract meaning from the way a person looks or acts as opposed to what that person said, or the ability to visualize the back of an object without having to rotate it in space. The ability to imagine what is not yet real, to innovate, and to solve problems is unique to the conscious mind.

To take full advantage of your conscious mind, focus on its care and feeding. Care for your brain through proper nutrition and exercise and by avoiding overindulgence in any substances that impair cognitive function. When you consciously choose to expose your brain to harmful substances in excess, you are choosing the substance over optimum cognitive function and, hence, over your desires, pursuits, relationships, and all the good available to you.

In addition, feed your conscious mind by exposing it to a wide variety of information, experiences, and challenges. Read and travel widely, take courses on topics of interest, engage in relationships with people from diverse backgrounds, pursue new hobbies and experiences. The greater the volume and variety of information your conscious mind has to draw from, the more creative and imaginative it will be, the better equipped it will be at solving problems, the more opportunities and options will appear on your mind's radar.

*Entrepreneur, university professor, and cofounder of Carbon, a
pioneer in the 3D printing industry, Joseph DeSimone delivers a
brief presentation entitled "Real Innovation Is Multidisciplinary,"
in which he explains how Apple founder Steve Jobs achieved
innovation through the convergence of social sciences, technology,
and the liberal arts. As part of his presentation, DeSimone quotes
Henry Rosovsky, dean emeritus of the Faculty of Arts and Science of
Harvard University, on the topic of research, faith, and innovation:*

*Research is an expression of faith in the possibility of progress.
The drive that leads scholars to study a topic has to include the belief
that new things can be discovered, that newer can be better, and
that greater depth of understanding is achievable. Research,
especially academic research, is a form of optimism about the
human condition.*

*DeSimone believes that a multidisciplinary approach—a
convergence of learning from different academic fields, including life
sciences (medicine), physical sciences, engineering, social sciences,
humanities, and perhaps even the performing arts—"is a blueprint
for innovation." The broader your education, experience, challenges,
and collaboration, the greater the potential for discovery.*

The Heart: Harness the Power of Your Emotions

Throughout this book, I stress the importance of emotions in transferring desires from the conscious to the subconscious mind. Specifically, I encourage you to use positive emotions (desire, faith, expectancy, gratitude, and so on) to transfer desires to the subconscious mind and avoid negative emotions (such as anxiety, fear, anger, and guilt), which tend to reinforce negative imagery. However, other positive emotions play a larger role when combined with the faculties of conscious thought and action—emotions such as confidence, enthusiasm, determination, enjoyment, and pride. It is these emotions, along with others, that provide the impetus and energy for action.

What often separates success from failure is determination, tenacity. In sports, the athlete or team that often wins, all other factors being relatively equal, is the one with the greater desire for victory. That desire energizes them, inspires them to train harder, and heightens their senses and performance. More importantly, perhaps, it provides them with a "failure is not an option" mentality.

The same is true with any endeavor or challenge. For example, if you examine people in long-term relationships, the most successful are those who make a commitment to one another and are serious about making their relationship work, regardless of how challenging that may be.

Kentucky Fried Chicken (KFC) is the world's second largest restaurant chain after McDonald's, with over 23,000 KFC outlets in more than 140 countries and territories around the world, but it wasn't an overnight success. Colonel Sanders did not start KFC until after he had turned sixty years old and collected his first Social Security check. He then had to drive across the United States from restaurant to restaurant cooking batches of chicken for hundreds of restaurant owners and their employees in an attempt to find someone to purchase his chicken recipe. He spent many nights on the road, often sleeping in his car, and received over a thousand rejections before anyone said yes.

By 1964, at the age of seventy-four, Colonel Sanders had more than six hundred franchised outlets for his chicken in the United States and Canada, and he sold his interest in the U.S. company for

$2 million (over $16 million in 2020 dollars) and lived the rest of his life in comfort, without having to depend on the meager, fixed income from Social Security.

Persistence is the key that unlocks the solution to overcoming many challenges. It wins wars, pays the mortgage, and saves investors from losing billions of dollars in market downturns when everyone else panics. It empowers engineers and construction workers to tunnel through mountains, build bridges over waterways, span continents with railways, and erect skyscrapers to dizzying heights. It drives medical researchers to engage in never-ending pursuits of treatments and cures for every ailment imaginable. It inspires and energizes those with artistic and musical talent to invest years in honing their craft, often with no guarantee of career or commercial success.

Nothing can substitute for persistence—not money, not education, not any advantage gained from birth or background or influential connections. Persistence is a personality trait, and it is often the equalizer between the rich and the poor. While the rich often become complacent from comfort, the poor develop persistence in the face of adversity. Those who achieve the greatest accomplishments often have persistence at their core, even though they may be lacking in talent, education, and financial means. And regardless of their peculiarities and shortcomings, they find a way to get things done. Hard work doesn't tire them, setbacks don't discourage them, and naysayers cannot divert them from their course. The most determined among us have achieved more success through sheer determination than others have with plenty of startup capital. Determination has overcome the most severe poverty and disability.

Those who are committed to victory never consider a defeat final. They rise from each defeat and every setback with a greater resolve, and they persist until they win. The words "can't" and "impossible" are not part of their vocabulary. Instead of being discouraged and disheartened by misfortune, they are inspired and invigorated by it.

Those who claim the greatest accomplishments are the most resilient. Those with little or no appetite for risk or tolerance for hardships, those who are unable to delay gratification, set less ambitious goals and are satisfied with lesser achievements.

Whenever you start to feel discouraged or are tempted to quit or turn back, reconsider. You may be standing just at the crest of a mountain over which you cannot see. By taking just a few steps forward, you may begin to see beyond the last major obstacle in your path to the downhill slope. Many of the major accomplishments and innovations of the past have occurred after less persistent individuals would have quit or turned back. The lives of those who lack the tenacity to complete challenging tasks are often a series of broken dreams, unfulfilled desires, and personal and professional failures. Don't let disappointment dull your ambition or enthusiasm. Persist!

The Hand: Act

The mind (conscious and subconscious) is the source of creativity, but creation requires more than thought; it requires action. Engaging the power of the subconscious mind alone may or may not be enough to obtain the object of your desire. In some cases, it will be enough; for example, suppose you want a piano and you pass your desire to your subconscious mind. Two days later, your neighbor informs you that she's moving out and asks, "Do you know anyone who wants a piano?" She tells you that she's moving to a smaller place, doesn't have room for it, never plays it, and just "wants to get rid of it." You don't even have to move it because the movers are there and would be happy to do it for you.

On the other hand, suppose you have a burning desire to play the piano. If you have an incredible talent for playing or are so in tune with the Divine that musicality is inspired, you may be able to sit down at the piano, play any arrangement imaginable, and even compose your own music. If you're like most people, though, you would need to invest some serious study and practice to learn how to play and how to read and compose music. That's not to say that study and practice would feel burdensome; if you're passionate about playing and composing music, the study and practice may feel effortless. Yet, it requires action and some degree of effort on your part.

Thought without action is the rock on which many novices in the New Thought movement wreck their ships. Thinking oneself rich doesn't necessarily, by itself, make one so. If you impress a desire upon the subconscious, action is necessary, either on your part or the part of others. In some cases, other people do most of the heavy lifting. In other cases, you may need to put out more of an effort or at least coordinate the work and resources required, serving in more of a management role.

Some individuals are more advanced than others in terms of their psychic powers. They can command Divine Energy and Matter directly, molding it like clay into their objects of desire. Most of us, however, must complement thought with action, using our physical faculties (our "hands") to do or delegate the work and procure the necessary materials and machinery. Ransom Olds did not merely invent the assembly line; he also patented the idea and took the steps necessary to have it implemented in his manufacturing plants. He may not have implemented it himself, but he had to delegate the work or collaborate with others. It could not have implemented itself.

Your job is not to guide or supervise the subconscious creative process, but you may need to be more hands-on with the conscious creative process. During the subconscious stage, all you need to do is retain your vision and maintain a mind-set of faith, expectation, and gratitude. When the subconscious mind, in concert with Divine Intelligence and Infinite Abundance, delivers the object of your desire or the opportunity to obtain it, your role changes. At this point, you need to receive the gift. You must act to appropriate what is yours and put it to work for you. *By subconscious thought, the gift is delivered to you; by conscious thought and action, the gift is received by you.* You are not likely to be the recipient of a magic machine with an endless supply of money. Some effort is likely to be required on your part.

> *When Jan Koum sold his company WhatsApp to Facebook for $19 billion in 2014, he chose to sign the deal a few blocks from WhatsApp's headquarters in Mountain View, California, in a building where he used to stand in line to collect food stamps. (WhatsApp is a cross-platform smartphone application that allows users to exchange text and voice messages, make voice and video calls, and share images, documents, user locations, and other media.)*
>
> *In 1992, at the age of sixteen, Koum and his mother and grandmother immigrated to Mountain View from a small village outside Kiev, Ukraine. In the United States, Koum's mother babysat and he cleaned at a local grocery store to cover the bills. (His father became ill and died in Ukraine in 1997, never making it to the U.S.)*

By eighteen, Koum had taught himself computer networking by studying manuals he had purchased from a used bookstore and returned when he was done with them. He enrolled at San Jose State University to study math and computer science while working at Ernst & Young as a security tester. In 1997, Koum was hired by Yahoo! as an infrastructure engineer, where he met Brian Acton, cofounder of WhatsApp. Koum quit school shortly thereafter.

Over the next nine years, Koum and Acton worked together at Yahoo! and then left the company in 2007, taking a year off to travel around South America. Both applied to work at Facebook and were rejected.

In 2009, Koum bought an iPhone and recognized the incredible potential of smartphone apps. He visited his friend Alex Fishman, and they talked for hours about Koum's idea for a more robust messaging app to provide users with an alternative to iPhone's short messaging service (SMS). Initially, WhatsApp wasn't very popular, but after Apple added a push notification and Koum added a feature to "ping" users when they received a message, the app began to gain popularity.

In February 2014, Facebook founder Mark Zuckerberg had Koum over to his home for dinner, where he asked Koum to join the Facebook board of directors. Ten days later, Facebook announced that it was acquiring WhatsApp.

As you can see from this story, except for the year or so he spent in South America, Koum was constantly doing something productive (acting). He was studying, working, meeting people, discussing ideas, and so on. Divine Intelligence and Infinite Abundance certainly provided him with opportunities, but without conscious thought and directed action on his part, and the part of his mother, Jan Koum may never have achieved the phenomenal success he experienced.

Do not wait to act. Act now. You cannot act in the past or future. The past is gone, the future has not yet arrived, waiting is not a suitable action, and you cannot plan how you will act in response to a future contingency until that contingency is present. Acting now means acting in response to current conditions. For example, if you have a certain interest or are drawn to a certain career, look into it, talk with others about it, read a book on the topic. If your desire is career or business oriented, take an entry-level job or pursue an internship in the field that interests you. Don't postpone action until a career change occurs or the desired business opportunity arises; start taking concrete steps to make the transition. Perhaps most of all, do not worry about what might go wrong; have faith that you are equipped to overcome any challenge that might arise.

> Do not wait to act. Act now.

Here are some suggestions to guide your action:

+ Waste no time daydreaming; envision what you desire and act *now*.

+ Take the initiative. Do not wait around for conditions, people, or your situation to change.

+ Do not worry about yesterday's work or mistakes you made in the past. Nobody can change the past.

+ Do your best work now to ensure the best possible tomorrow.

+ Envision yourself in the better situation but take action to improve it or be transferred to a better situation.

+ Do not look for a remarkable or unconventional step to take to become wealthy. Your actions probably will be the same as those you have been performing for some time but with a more positive attitude and greater certainty of success.

+ Do not feel discouraged if positive change comes slowly. Discouragement is a symptom of negative thinking, which will result in lack and limitation.

+ Use your present career, business, or situation as the means to get a better one. Do not make any drastic decisions unless compelled to do so by conscious or subconscious thought (good reasons or strong intuition).

+ If you are an employee dissatisfied with your current position, focus on being the best employee you can be. Dissatisfaction will only undermine your ability to gain a better position. Hold the vision of yourself in the job you want, while you *act* to deliver the greatest value to your current employer.

+ Your vision and faith will set the creative force in motion to bring your desired career or business opportunity toward you, while your action will cause the forces in your current environment to move you toward the place you want.

The notion of acting in the present, in your current situation, is based on the fact that advancement occurs only by those who expand beyond their current positions. Nobody is going to offer you a raise, a promotion, or an opportunity until you prove yourself more valuable than the position you currently hold or the business you own or manage. When you take action to bring more value to your current position or customers, you expand beyond that position or business and attract more lucrative and rewarding opportunities.

People who fail to fill their current positions begin to move backward, as you can observe when employees are fired or laid off. When people do not fill their current positions, they become a drag on their employer, their family, society, and government. Society can advance only when its members expand beyond their current positions, increasing the value they deliver and creating opportunities for others.

Chapter Takeaways

+ To optimize your success in getting what you desire, engage all three human faculties—head (conscious mind), heart (subconscious mind and emotions), and hand (ability to act).

+ The conscious mind has four essential functions: attention, reasoning/analysis, decision, and imagination.

+ Your brain is the temple of your subconscious and conscious minds. Care for it through proper nutrition and exercise and by avoiding excess consumption of alcohol and other substances that negatively impact cognitive function. Feed it a large volume and variety of information and experience.

+ Your heart is the source of your emotions. It provides the energy needed to imprint desires upon the subconscious mind and the determination and confidence to take action.

+ Tenacity often makes the difference between failure and success. Those who claim the greatest accomplishments are often the most persistent.

+ Persistence can overcome many other perceived limitations, including limited education, startup capital, and influential connections.

+ Creativity and success require more than just thought; they require action.

+ Though action is required to bring a desire or idea to fruition, you may or may not need to invest a great deal of effort; often, you do, but sometimes the object of your desire arrives with little or no effort.

+ By subconscious thought, the gift is delivered to you; by conscious thought and action, the gift is received by you.

CHAPTER 10

Live a Fulfilling Life

◆

Growing rich is about much more than attaining wealth and physical possessions. It involves good health, strong personal and professional relationships, self-fulfillment, and intellectual, emotional, and spiritual development. When you begin to harness the power of your subconscious mind, you begin to reap the benefits in all facets of your life. You begin to live life joyously, feeling truly happy and alive.

People often wonder, "What is the purpose of life?" Some believe that a Supreme Being has a master plan for the universe and an individual plan for each of us—that our lives are predestined or that we are given a choice to live according to the plan (and be happy) or to disregard that plan and (presumably) live in misery either here on earth or in the afterlife due to our disobedience. Some believe that life has no purpose or meaning or that each of us is responsible for defining life's meaning and our purpose on earth for ourselves. Others believe that we should work hard and sacrifice for others in this life to earn rewards and avoid punishment in an afterlife.

When you contemplate the Divine, you begin to realize that the purpose of life is to fully live it and enjoy it. Divine Intelligence is a Creative Force that permeates all being, seen and unseen. It continuously strives toward a more complete expression of itself, at least partially through us. As extensions of the Divine, our purpose is the full realization of our potential—to be, have, and do to our maximum capacity, to fully express who we are and to fully enjoy the bounty that surrounds us.

Consider anyone who is the best at what they do or the top in their field. These individuals are usually very passionate about what they do, and they have invested heavily in pursuing their passions. We deem them successful, and they are typically very wealthy, even though most of them never actively pursued wealth. They pursued a passion that subsequently enriched the lives of others in a way and to a degree that earned them riches.

Focus your consciousness on the fact that the desire you feel for the possession of riches is one with the desire of Omnipotence for more complete expression, and your faith becomes invincible.

A Pattern for Divine Living

On Thanksgiving Day, I flew to the island of Kauai to mingle with residents and see the sights. I met a guide who introduced me to many of his friends and took me to several houses on the island to see how they live. I found the people in the homes I visited to be happy, joyous, and free. They are kind, generous, deeply spiritual, and full of the music and laughter of God. I found myself looking at people who are living life gloriously in the spirit of Divine Liberty.

In making a few purchases in one remote village here on Kauai,

I had an interesting conversation with a man who came from the mainland some years ago and who is now running a country store. His wife had deserted him and had taken all the money with her. Although he was well-aware of his own shortcomings as a husband, he had become bitter, irascible, and hateful and had found great difficulty in meshing into an organization. A friend suggested that he go to Kauai, explaining to him that it was the oldest island of the Hawaiian chain and that it basks in rare beauty, full of lush foliage and floral growth. His friend told him of the deep colorful canyons, golden beaches, and winding rivers, all of which captured his imagination.

He worked in the sugarcane fields here for some months. One day he fell ill and was confined to a hospital for several weeks. Each day the Hawaiian people visited him, brought him fruit, prayed for him, and showed a deep interest in his welfare. Their kindness, love, and attention penetrated his heart, and he reciprocated by pouring out love, peace, and goodwill to them. He became a transformed man.

This man's formula is very simple; it is that love will always triumph over hate, and goodness will always triumph over evil, for that is the way the universe is made. I would like to comment on what transpired psychologically and spiritually in this case. This man's heart was corroded with bitterness, self-condemnation, and hatred. The love, kindness, and prayers of his fellow workers penetrated the layers of his subconscious mind, expunging all the negative patterns lodged therein, and his heart became full of love and goodwill to all. He discovered that love is the universal solvent. His constant affirmation now is, "I pour out Divine Love, Peace, and Joy to every person I meet every day of my life." The more love he gives, the more he receives. To give is more blessed than to receive.

Every morning when you open your eyes, affirm boldly and with deep feeling and understanding:

1. I rejoice and give thanks that my life is directed by the same Eternal Wisdom which guides the planets in their courses and causes the sun to shine.

2. I am going to live life gloriously today and every day. I experience more and more Divine Love, Light, Truth, and Beauty all day long today and every day.

3. I am going to be of tremendous help to all those whom I contact and with whom I work, and I will have the time of my life doing it.

4. I am going to be deeply enthusiastic about my work and my wonderful opportunities for service.

5. I rejoice and give thanks that I experience and manifest more and more of Divine Glory each and every day.

Begin each day by affirming these miraculous truths and believe in their reality. Whatever you believe and faithfully anticipate will come to pass, and wonders will happen in your life.

To Own All and Own Nothing

I met an extraordinary man at the Fern Grotto, where the boat crew is noted for singing the never-forgotten Hawaiian Wedding Song. He was ninety-six years old, walked briskly, and sang on the boat with gusto the beautiful Hawaiian love songs as we traveled to the famous Grotto. After the trip, he invited me to his home, which was indeed a rare experience. For dinner we had thickly sliced homemade gingerbread, papaya, apple tart, rice, broiled salmon, and Kona coffee grown on one of the neighboring islands.

During dinner he told me how he had become a new man through his connection with the Divine, and at ninety-six he certainly looked the part. His cheeks were ruddy with radiant and buoyant health; his eyes were filled with light and love; joy was all over his face. He spoke fluently English, Spanish, Chinese, Japanese, and Hawaiian. He regaled me with as fine a flood of native wisdom, witticisms, jokes, and good humor as I had ever heard.

I was thoroughly fascinated and finally asked him, "Tell me your secret of life and joy. You seem to be bubbling over with enthusiasm and energy." "Why shouldn't I be happy and strong?" he replied. "You see, I own the island and yet I own nothing." He added, "God possesses everything, but the whole island and all that is in it is mine to enjoy—the mountains, the rivers, the caves, the people, and the rainbows. Do you know where I got this home?" he asked, and he answered himself, saying, "A grateful traveler bought it for me and gave it to me as a gift; otherwise, I wouldn't have it."

He added that about sixty years ago he was dying of tuberculosis and had been given up as hopeless, but a local Kahuna (native priest) visited him and told both him and his mother that he would live through a spiritual healing. The Kahuna chanted prayers, placed his hands on his throat and chest, and in his native tongue called on Divine Healing Power. At the end of about an hour's chanting, he said he was completely healed, and the next day he went fishing. Since then, he said, "I've never had a pain or an ache of any kind. I have marvelous legs. I've walked all over these mountains you see. Moreover," he concluded, "I have kind, loving friends, a few dogs and goats, and this wonderful island. And I have God in my heart. Why shouldn't I be happy and strong?"

This remarkable man tills his land, takes care of his goats and sheep, visits the sick, attends all the festivals, and sings Hawaiian love songs which touch the soul. His secret? He owns everything, yet he owns nothing; he allows the abundant life to flow through him and around him. He is not interested in storing up riches on earth but in using Infinite Abundance to enrich his life and the lives of others.

Knowing the laws of mind, you can readily see the impression his Kahuna priest made upon him. He had absolute faith in the powers of the Kahuna, and he believed implicitly that he would be healed. According to his belief, his subconscious mind responded.

The process of aligning one's mind with Divine Abundance can be summed up in one word, *gratitude*. First, you believe in Divine Abundance; second, you believe that Divine Intelligence fulfills all your needs and desires; and third, you deepen your connection with the Source through a feeling of profound gratitude.

Many people who have used the power of their subconscious mind successfully at one time fall back into poverty through their lack of gratitude. After claiming and receiving a generous gift, they fail to express their gratitude to the Source, thus breaking their connection to and distancing themselves from the Source.

Keep in mind that the nearer you remain to the Source, the more good things will flow to you and through you, and you remain closer through the Source when you maintain a grateful mind-set. An ever-present sense of gratitude benefits you in three ways:

+ Maintains your connection to the Source after you have received that which you desired.

+ Crowds out any thoughts of lack, limitation, or doubt. Faith is born of gratitude. The grateful mind is a mind full of expectation, and expectation is faith. Every outgoing wave of grateful thanksgiving is an expression of faith.

+ Draws the Source closer to you. Your expression of gratitude is an expenditure of energy toward the Source which prompts an equal and opposite reaction toward you—driving more of all that is good toward you.

Don't waste your time, energy, and mindpower complaining about big business or corporate executives earning too much money or becoming successful due to low taxes or the hard work of underpaid employees. Corporations of the world create opportunities for workers. It is the rich that are often the biggest investors in new ideas and business ventures that create new opportunities.

In a democratic society, feel free to protest injustice and vote politicians out of office whom you believe are corrupt or incompetent or are in favor of policies that could harm the country. However, don't waste your time and energy thinking and talking about the shortcomings of politicians or government in general. If it weren't for some degree of government control and law and order, the country would fall into anarchy, greatly diminishing opportunities for everyone.

Have faith that Infinite Intelligence is gradually making the world a better place, increasing opportunities, and raising the standard of living. Be grateful for government and industrial leaders who provide the infrastructure, safety, and opportunities for growth and development. Affirm daily that they grow in wisdom and goodness. As a result, you will align yourself with the Creative Force and Substance that produces all things good.

Henry David Thoreau said, "We should give thanks that we were born." Practice living each day filled with sincere gratitude and thanksgiving. As you do, your appreciation and anticipation of good will find a way by repetition to the deeper layers of your mind, and, like seeds, they will grow after their kind. Let wonders happen in your life.

In Touch with Divine Intelligence

I have found that the Hawaiians are very wise people, having acquired through centuries a vast accumulation of esoteric and unwritten knowledge. One man, an indigenous native of Maui who sat next to me on the plane from Kauai to Maui, had knowledge of weather conditions, currents, tides, and so on. He informed me that he could predict tidal waves, storms, and volcanic eruptions. He knows by name all the fruits, flowers, and trees in the islands and understands the curative properties of the herbs.

He has the capacity to read minds and is clairvoyant. He told me where I was going, gave my name and address, and had the gift of retrocognition, as he spoke most accurately of many past events in my life. To test his gift of clairvoyance, I asked him to read a letter which was in my pocket, which I had not read, having forgotten all about it until that moment. He read the contents accurately, as my subsequent reading verified.

This young man is in touch with his subconscious mind, which knows the answers to all questions. "Whenever I want to know something," he said, "I just say, 'God, you know. Tell me.' The answer always comes, because I have a friend inside." This man works in the cane fields, plays the ukulele, sings at his work, and obviously is in tune with the Infinite. Truly, he has a friend inside and he has discovered the joy of the Divine Presence which is his strength.

How to Acquire the Joy of Living

I have been in correspondence with a young woman on Kauai whom I will call Jenny. She wrote to report that she was full of fear and in deep distress.

She had broken her engagement to a young man, and he had retaliated by informing her that a Kahuna had cursed her. She lived in constant fear. I wrote to her explaining that there is only One Power, and that this Power moves as unity and harmony in the world; that this Supreme Being is Spirit, One and Indivisible; and that one part of Spirit could not be antagonistic to another part of Spirit; therefore, there was nothing to fear. I wrote out a spiritual technique for her to follow, which would banish all fear.

In my interview with her, I detected a radiant personality, a young woman exuding vibrancy, bubbling over with enthusiasm and joy, and on fire with new ideas for the island. She said, "I followed your instructions to the letter and I am transformed by an inner light."

The following is the spiritual regimen she practiced several times daily, as suggested in my letter to her:

Divine Being is all there is. One with the Almighty is a majority. With the Almighty on my side, nothing can stand in my way. I know and believe in the Eternal One, Divine Power, Divine Intelligence—and there is no power to challenge It. I know and accept completely that when my thoughts are Divine Thoughts, Divine Power is with my thoughts of good. I know I cannot receive what I cannot give, and I give out thoughts of love, peace, light, and goodwill to my ex-boyfriend and all those connected with him. I am immunized and intoxicated with the Holy Spirit, and I am always surrounded by the sacred circle of Divine Love. The whole armor of the Almighty surrounds me and enfolds me. I am divinely guided and directed, and I enter into the joy of living.

She practiced repeating these truths regularly and systematically for about ten minutes morning, afternoon, and night, knowing, believing, and understanding that as she affirmed these truths they would gradually sink into her subconscious mind by a process of spiritual osmosis and come forth as freedom, inner peace, a sense of security, confidence, and protection. She knew she was applying a law of mind which never fails. In ten days' time all fear vanished. Now she has a wonderful position here on the island. She introduced me to her new boyfriend, and his comment was, "She is the joy of my life." This young woman who had been practically petrified by fear of a supposed curse is now out-flowing, giving of her talents, and has entered into the joy of living.

The Meaning of "Kahuna"

Kahuna is a Hawaiian word for medicine man or shaman who generally heals and casts good spells through his incantations and esoteric knowledge. One of my Hawaiian guides explained to me that these wise and gifted Kahunas were trained from early child-hood by their indigenous elders, who subjected them to severe dis-cipline and secrecy. Many of them are highly respected for their healing powers through what we would call today knowledge of the subconscious mind. They have, also, a deep knowledge of the curative properties of certain herbs and plants passed down through generations as part of their remarkable indigenous culture.

The above-mentioned woman learned that the threats, negative suggestions, and statements of others have absolutely no power to create the things they suggest. You are the only thinker in your universe. It is your thought that is creative. Think good and good follows; think evil and evil follows. Join with Supreme Being. When your thoughts are Divine Thoughts, Divine Power is with your thoughts of good. Remember that one with the Almighty is a majority, and that with the Almighty on your side, nothing can stand in your way.

Chapter Takeaways

+ Loving the Supreme Being, which means loving goodness, purity, truth, and right action, enables you to live life gloriously.

+ Love is the universal solvent, dissolving any hatred, envy, or negativity in others and fostering love in the person to whom it is directed.

+ When you open your eyes in the morning, affirm gladly, "This is the day the Lord has made for me. I will rejoice and be glad in it. I give thanks that my life is directed by the same Divine Wisdom that guides the planets in their courses and causes the sun to shine."

+ Believe in Divine Guidance, and wonders will happen in your life.

+ Realize that age is not the flight of years, but the dawn of wisdom in your mind.

+ A grateful heart is always close to Divine Being.

+ To feel inspired and zestful all your life, remain conscious of the Divine Presence at all times.

+ You become what you contemplate. Contemplate eternal truths, such as those of Divine Abundance.

+ The powers of clairvoyance, precognition, mental telepathy, and astral projection are within you. As you grow in wisdom, you will begin to tap the infinite reservoir within you, and these latent faculties of the mind will become active in your life.

+ You cannot receive what you cannot give. This is a law of mind. Give love, joy, and goodwill to all. The more you give, the more blessings come to you.

Recharge Your Mental and Spiritual Batteries

◆

If you feel stressed out, burned out, or exhausted, it is time to recharge
your mental and spiritual batteries. A relaxing weekend or vacation may
help to some degree, but a more effective approach is to engage in
prayer or meditation. When you pray or meditate, you plug yourself
into the very source of your energy and strength—Divine Being.
It is like immersing yourself in a clear mountain stream in the
middle of summer!

Many businesspeople and professionals of different religious
persuasions regularly and periodically go on retreats where
they relax, meditate, and attend presentations delivered by inspira-
tional speakers. After a morning meditation, they are told to contemplate what they heard and remain silent for several days, even
during mealtimes. All this time they are encouraged to dwell
calmly and quietly on the instructions and meditations given each
morning.

All of them have told me that they come back renewed, refreshed,
and replenished spiritually and mentally. Following their return to

their offices, factories, and professional lives, they continue to maintain quiet periods for fifteen to twenty minutes daily, morning and evening, and they have found that they get more done as a result of being able to "quiet the mind"—shifting their focus from the five-sense material world to the spiritual world within them.

Having recharged their mental and spiritual batteries, these men and women are able to meet head on and, with faith, courage, and confidence, cope with the problems, strife, vexations, and contentions of the day. They know where and how to receive renewed spiritual power—by tuning in quietly, as Emerson says, with the Infinite, which lies stretched in smiling repose. Energy, power, inspiration, guidance, and wisdom come out of the silence and the stillness of the mind when tuned in to Divine Being. These men and women have learned to relax and to give up their egoistic pride. They have recognized, honored, and called upon a wisdom and power that created all things visible and invisible and that governs all things ceaselessly, timelessly, and forever. They have decided to go the way of wisdom.

The Quiet Mind Is within Your Reach

If I offer you a gift of a book, in order to receive it, you must reach for it by stretching forth your hand. In like manner, since all the riches of Divine Being are within you, you must make some effort to claim them. The Living Spirit is the giver and the gift, but you are the recipient. Open your mind and heart and let in the Divine River of Peace. Let it fill your mind and heart, for the Living Spirit is peace.

Meditate on the immeasurable nature of the universe to which we belong, the Infinite Mind and Infinite Intelligence, which created us and animates and supports us, and which moves rhythmically, harmoniously, ceaselessly, changelessly, and with mathematical precision, gives you faith, confidence, strength, and security. Know that you have dominion over your thoughts, feelings, actions, and reactions in life. This fills you with self-esteem and a sense of worthiness and power, which endows you with strength to do your work, live joyously, and walk the earth with praise for the Supreme Being forever on your lips.

Quiet the Mind in a Troubled World

Some time ago I had a conversation with a businessman, who finally said to me, "How can I get a quiet mind in a troubled and confused world? I know that it is said 'A quiet mind gets things done.' I'm confused and troubled, and the propaganda in the newspapers, radio, and television is driving me half-crazy."

I said to him that I would attempt to throw some light on his problem; provide him with spiritual medicine, which would allay his fears and anxieties; and give him the quiet mind which gets things done. I pointed out that if his thoughts morning, noon, and night revolved around war, crime, sickness, disease, accidents, and misfortune, he would automatically bring on the mood of depression, anxiety, and fear. But if, on the other hand, he gave some of his time and attention to the eternal laws and principles which govern the cosmos and all life, he would automatically be lifted up into the mental atmosphere of inner security and serenity.

As a result, three times a day this man filled his mind with the following truths:

> I know a Supreme Intelligence governs the planets in their courses and controls and directs the entire universe. I know there is Divine Law and Order operating with absolute certainty fashioning the entire world, causing the stars to come nightly to the sky and regulating the galaxies in space; and the Creator is ruling the universe. I move mentally into the stillness of my own mind and contemplate these Divine Eternal Truths.

This businessman turned away from the concerns and worries of the day and gave attention to the great principles and truths of life, contemplated them, and focused his attention on them. He forgot the little things and began to think about the great, the wonderful, and the good. When he turned away from the trials and troubles of the world and refused to describe them or even talk about them at any length, his anxiety and worry diminished and he developed a quiet mind in a troubled world. He decided to let Divine Peace rule in his heart. Consequently, his business ran smoother, driven by much better decisions which he could now make.

Calm Internal Conflict

One day in Beverly Hills, a man who recognized me stopped me on the street and said that he was terribly disturbed. He asked, "Do you think I can get a quiet mind? I have been at war with my-self for over two months." There was a conflict raging within him. He was full of fears, doubts, hates, and religious bigotry. He was furious because his daughter had married into a different faith, and he said that he hated her husband. He was not on speaking terms with his own son because the son joined the armed forces and he (the father) belonged to a peace crusade. And to top things off, his wife was suing him for divorce.

I was not able to give him much time on the street corner, but I told him briefly that he should be delighted that his daughter had married the man of her dreams and that, if they loved each other, they certainly should marry, as love knows no creed, race, dogma, or color. Love is Divine, and Divine Being is impersonal and no respecter of persons. Regarding his son, I suggested that he write the young man and tell him how much he loves him and to pray for him. I said he should respect his son's decision and not interfere with him other than to wish for him all the blessings of life. I also told him that I gathered from his conversation that the bickering and quarreling in their marriage was probably due to an unresolved childhood conflict with his mother and that he expected his wife to be a substitute for his mother.

I wrote down on a piece of paper these everlasting truths and gave them to him to read and digest: "You will keep him in perfect peace, whose mind is focused on You, because he trusts in You." I urged him to keep his mind focused on the Supreme Being with trust, faith, and certainty, and that he would then feel the river of life, love, and inner quiet filling his heart. I added that whenever he thought of anyone in his family, he was to say, "Divine Peace fills my soul and Divine Peace fills his or her soul."

A few days later I had a note from this man, which said, "Life was like hell for me. I hated to open my eyes in the morning. I took phenobarbital every night to sleep. After I left you on the street, though, I surrendered my family and myself to God and affirmed constantly: 'God will keep me in perfect peace, because my mind is stayed on Him.' The change that has come over me is unbeliev-able. Life has become full of joy and wonder.

"My wife canceled divorce proceedings, and we are back to-gether again. I wrote letters to my daughter and son-in-law and to my son, and we now live in peace, harmony, and understanding."

All that this man did was get all the hatred and resentment out of his heart. As he surrendered to the golden river of peace within, it flowed in response to him, and all the pieces fell into place in Di-vine Order.

How a "Victim of Circumstances" Stopped Being a Victim

During the summer months, I had the pleasure of conducting a seminar near Denver, Colorado. While there I interviewed a man who said, "I'm fenced in, frustrated, unhappy, and blocked at every turn of the road. I want to sell my ranch and get away, but I feel like I'm in jail—just stuck."

"Well," I said, "if I hypnotized you now, you would believe your-self to be whatever I suggested you were, because your conscious mind, which reasons and judges and weighs, would be suspended, and your subconscious mind, being noncontroversial, would accept whatever suggestion is given to it. If I suggested to you that you were an Indian guide and you were to track down a criminal, you would proceed stealthily to look for him in the mountains.

"If I told you you were in jail, you would feel yourself a prisoner and you would believe yourself in jail surrounded by walls and bars of steel. If I instructed you to try your best to escape, you would look for a way out. You might try to pick the lock, chisel out the mortar between the concrete blocks, or steal the keys from the prison guard. All the time you would be here in the wide-open spaces of Colorado as free as the wind. All this is due to the amenability of your subconscious to its suggestions, which it faithfully executes.

"Likewise, you have suggested to your subconscious mind that you can't sell the ranch, that you are a prisoner here, that you can't go to Denver and do what you want to do, that you are in debt, and that you are blocked at every turn. Your subconscious mind has no alternative but to accept the suggestions you give it, as it is oblivious to everything but that which you impress upon it.

"Actually, you have mesmerized and hypnotized yourself. Your bondage and restrictions are self-imposed, and you are suffering and in continuous mental conflict from your false opinions and beliefs."

I suggested he repent. To repent means to think again—to think from the standpoint of basic principles and eternal verities. I told him to stand up boldly and claim his good, for, as Shakespeare said, "All things are ready if the mind be so." I added that he had to ready and prepare his mind to receive his good now, for the kingdom of harmony, health, peace, guidance, abundance, and security is at hand, waiting only for him to accept and take his good now.

The prescription I handed this man consisted of the following affirmation to be repeated daily:

> My mind is now absorbed, interested, and fascinated in the eternal, changeless truths of Divine Being. I now still my mind and contemplate the great truth that the Living Spirit dwells in

me and walks and talks in me. I still the wheels of my mind and know that the Living Spirit dwells in me. I know this and believe it.

Infinite Intelligence draws the buyer who wants my ranch, he prospers in it, there is a Divine exchange, and we are both blessed. The buyer is right and the price is right, and the deeper currents of my subconscious mind bring both of us together in Divine Order. I know that *all things are ready if the mind be so.* When worrisome thoughts come to my mind, I will immediately affirm, "None of these things moves me." I know I am reconditioning my mind to stillness, relaxation, equanimity, and imperturbability. I am making a new world of freedom, abundance, and security for myself.

A few weeks later I had a telephone call from this rancher telling me that he had sold his ranch and was thus free to go to Denver. He was no longer a prisoner of his mind. He said, "I realized I put myself in a prison of want, limitation, and restriction by my negative thinking and that, actually, I was self-hypnotized."

This man learned that his thought was creative and that all his frustration was due to the suggestions of others, which he accepted, although he could have rejected them, and that events, circumstances, and conditions were not causative. They suggested fears and limitations, which he indulged instead of completely rejecting them, realizing that straight-line thinking was the only cause and power in his world. His repeated meditation gave him power to think constructively and proved to him his capacity to choose wisely from universal principles.

When anxieties, worries, and fears come to you, maintain your inner equilibrium and affirm, "I will lift up my eyes to the Living

Spirit, who gives me strength. No outside events or circumstances can move me."

Chapter Takeaways

+ Stop thinking about the calamities in the world—the crimes, disasters, sickness, political upheaval, and tragedies. Realize that Divine Law and Order govern the world, and you will be lifted above the malevolence and chaos caused by the turbulent and negative mass mind.

+ Mentally retreat into the stillness of your mind and contemplate the undeviating laws and principles behind all things. Keep your mind on Divine Being and you will possess serenity and all you desire.

+ Stop thinking about and talking about symptoms, troubles, and worries. That which you feed only grows stronger.

+ As you turn your mind and heart to the Divine, any anger and animosity you may feel will dissolve.

+ Cosmic Good is the giver and the gift. You are the recipient. Reach out mentally now to let the river of peace flow through your heart and mind. Divine Presence is the eternal now. Why wait for it? Accept it *now!*

+ Love transcends all religious and institutional dogma. Do not allow difference in religion or politics to get in the way of love.

+ You are not a victim of circumstances, conditions, heredity, or environment. These cannot control you, but through the power of your subconscious mind, you can control or transcend them.

CHAPTER 12

Let Divine Intelligence Guide
You in All Ways

◆

Some people are blessed with the power of intuition; they always seem
to be at the right place at the right time and know just what to do to
capitalize on opportunities. Intuition is a power of the subconscious
mind. As such, it is available to anyone who is receptive to it. By
learning to harness the power of your subconscious mind, you become
the beneficiary of Divine Guidance—an Intelligent Force that protects
you and leads you to all things good.

There is a principle of Divine Guidance operating in you and throughout the universe, and by using the Infinite Intelligence within you, you can attract many wonderful experiences and happenings beyond your most ambitious dreams. This chapter will reveal to you the principles of Divine Guidance in a variety of ways, so that you may apply them to attract all kinds of blessings into your life.

Divine Guidance Leads to Right Action

Divine Guidance comes when your motives are right, and when your real inner desire is to do the right thing. When your thought is right—that is, when it conforms to the Golden Rule and the law of goodwill for all—a feeling of inner peace and tranquility wells up within you. This inner feeling of poise, balance, and equanimity causes you to do the right thing in all phases of your life. When you sincerely wish for others what you wish for yourself, then you are practicing love, which is the fulfillment of the law of health, happiness, and peace of mind.

A friend of mine, a builder, is always busy and can't adequately handle all his business calls. He said to me, "They tell me the building business is slow, but I can't keep up with the calls." He added that he had made lots of mistakes in the past and had lost two small fortunes in bad ventures, but six years ago he began to use affirmations to engage the power of his subconscious mind. He showed me his daily affirmation typed neatly on a card, which he carries with him all the time. It read as follows:

> I forgive myself for all the mistakes of the past. I blame no one. All my mistakes were stepping-stones to my success, prosperity, and advancement. I believe implicitly that the Living Spirit is guiding me always and that whatever I do will be right. I go forward confidently without fear. I give the best that is in me to all my work. I feel, believe, claim, and know that I am lifted up, guided, directed, sustained, prospered, and protected in all ways. I do the right thing, I think the right thoughts, and I know there is an Infinite Intelligence in my subconscious mind that answers me. I give the best to my customers. I am guided to give the right price, and I am inspired to see what is to be done

and I do it. I attract the right workers, who labor harmoniously
with me. I know these thoughts sink into my subconscious mind
forming a subjective pattern, and I believe I will get an
automatic response from my subconscious mind in accordance
with my habitual thinking.

This is the builder's daily affirmation, and he is automatically
guided to all good. He said to me that everything he does seems to
have the touch of Midas, the Golden Touch for prosperity. He has
had no errors, losses, or labor disputes in over six years. Truly, he
is automatically guided, as you can be too.

Remember, your subconscious mind responds to the nature of
your conscious mind's thinking and imagery.

The late Dr. Harry Gaze, author of *Emmet Fox, The Man and His
Work*, believed in the principle of Divine Guidance in all his undertakings. One time he was about to board a plane, and an inner
voice told him not to go. His bags were on the plane already, but
he had them taken off and canceled the trip. He followed this in-
tuitive impulse, and it saved his life because all those on that plane
were lost.

Find Your True Place in Life

You build up confidence and trust in the Infinite Guiding Force by
knowing that Divine Being is Infinite Life and that you are eternal
life made manifest. The Life Principle is interested in seeking expression through you. You are unique and entirely different. You
think, speak, and act differently. There is no one in all the world
like you. The Life Principle never repeats Itself. Realize, know,

and believe that you have special and unique talents and capabili-
ties. You can do something in a special way that no one else in all
the world can do because you are you. You are here to express
yourself fully and to do what you love to do, thereby fulfilling your
destiny in life. You are important. You are an organ or expression
of the Divine. You are needed where you are; otherwise, you would
not be here. Divine Presence dwells in you. All the powers, attributes, and qualities of the Divine are within you. You have faith,
imagination, and the power to choose and think. You mold, fashion, and create your own destiny by the way you think.

How Divine Guidance Revealed True Talents

A young man who had struggled in the musical field, in the theater as an actor, and in business also, said to me, "I have failed in
everything." I suggested to him that the answer to his problem was
within himself and that he could find out his true expression in
life. I explained to him that when he was doing what he loved to
do, he would be happy, successful, and prosperous.

At my suggestion, he affirmed as follows:

> I have the power to rise higher in life. I have now come to a
> clear-cut decision that I was born to succeed and lead a
> triumphant, constructive life. I have reached the inner
> conviction that the royal road to success is mine now. Infinite
> Intelligence within me reveals my hidden talents, and I follow
> the lead which comes into my conscious, reasoning mind. I
> recognize it clearly. Success is mine now. Wealth is mine. I am
> doing what I love to do, and I am serving humanity in a

wonderful way. I believe in the Principle of Guidance, and I know the answer comes, as it is done unto me as I believe.

After a few weeks of repeating this affirmation several times daily and with complete faith, this young man had an intense desire to study for the ministry along the lines of the Science of the Mind. Today he is a tremendous success as a teacher, minister, and counselor, and he is immensely happy in his work. He discovered an Infinite Guiding Principle that knew his inner talents and revealed them to him according to his belief.

How a Fortune in Mind Was Discovered by an Eighty-Year-Old Woman

I had a most interesting conversation with a woman over eighty years of age who is alert, mentally alive, illumined, inspired, and quickened by the Divine Spirit, which animates her entire being. She told me that for several weeks she had asked her Higher Self prior to sleep, "My Higher Self reveals to me a new idea, which is complete in my mind and which I can visualize with the greatest facility. This idea blesses all people." She was given the complete model of an invention as an image in her mind. She in turn gave the drawing to her son, who is an engineer, and he submitted it to a patent attorney, who had it patented. She has been offered $50,000 by one organization for the patent, plus a percentage of the sales.

She believed that the Supreme Intelligence within her, the Infinite Guiding Principle, would respond, and that the idea would be complete, including every possible improvement needed. Her

> The answer to all things is already within you.

directive was carried out just as she had expected, visualized, and planned.

Regardless of your profession, business, trade, or occupation, *you* have the power to still your mind and call upon the Infinite Intelligence of your subconscious to reveal to you a new idea that will bless you and the world. You can firmly believe that you will secure an answer. The answer to all things is already within you. It was there from the foundation of time. Divine Intelligence dwells in you and knows the answer.

A Dream Come True

A young boy, aged twelve, who listens to my morning radio program, told his mother that he was going to visit his uncle in Australia during school vacation. His thought of going was very strong, but he had another thought which said, "Mom won't let me go." His mother had said, "It's impossible. We don't have the money, and your father can't possibly afford it. You're dreaming."

Her son said, however, that he heard on my radio program that if you desired to do something and believed that the Creative Intelligence within you would bring it to pass, your desire would be fulfilled. His mother said, "Go ahead and try." This boy, who had been reading extensively about Australia and New Zealand, had an uncle in Australia who owned a big ranch. The boy affirmed as follows: "Creative Intelligence opens up the way for Dad, Mom, and me to go to Australia during vacation. I believe this and the

Creative Force takes over now." When the thought that his parents didn't have the money to go came to his mind, he would affirm, "Creative Intelligence opens up the way." His thoughts came in pairs, but he gave attention to the constructive thought, and the negative thought died away.

One night, he had a dream wherein he found himself on his uncle's ranch in New South Wales, viewing thousands of sheep, and meeting his uncle and cousins. When he awakened the next morning, he described the entire scene to his mother, much to her amazement. The same day, a letter came from his uncle inviting the three of them to his ranch and offering to defray their expenses both ways. They accepted.

The boy's intense desire to visit his uncle acted on his subconscious mind as a command while asleep; and, using his fourth-dimensional body, he traveled astrally to the ranch. The boy told me that what he observed when he arrived at the ranch with his parents coincided exactly with what he saw in his astral projection while asleep. Thus, it was done unto him as he believed.

Use Infinite Power to Guide Others

You can use the Infinite Power to guide someone other than yourself, whether the other is a stranger, relative, or close friend. You can do this by knowing that the Infinite Guiding Power is responsive to your thought and by believing in this Infinite response. I have done this for many people with extraordinary and fascinating results.

For example, a young engineer called me on the phone one day and said, "The organization I am with is selling out to a larger firm, and I am told I am not needed in the new setup. Would you pray for Divine Guidance for me?" I told him that there was an Infinite Guiding Principle which would reveal a new door of expression for him, and all that he had to do was to believe that this is so in the same way that he believed in Boyle's law or Avogadro's law in science.

I used the principle as follows: I pictured this engineer saying to me, "I found a wonderful position with a wonderful salary. It came to me 'out of the blue.'" I did this for about three or four minutes after he hung up the phone and then forgot all about it. I believed and expected an answer.

The following day he called me and confirmed the fact that he had accepted a good offer with a new engineering firm. The offer, he said, came to him "out of the blue"!

There is but one Mind, and what I subjectively pictured and felt as true came to pass in the experience of the engineer. When you call upon the Infinite Guiding Principle, It always answers you. What you believe will take place will surely happen.

Chapter Takeaways

+ Learn from your mistakes; they are stepping-stones to your success.

+ There is a Divine Guidance that responds to your belief in It.

+ You can harness the power of Divine Intelligence to guide others through the One Divine Mind. Your vision and belief in the other person's welfare are communicated instantly to the other person's subconscious, which works to bring a positive outcome to fruition.

+ To discover your hidden talents and your true calling, enlist the aid of Divine Intelligence by affirming with conviction, "Divine Intelligence reveals my hidden talents to me and opens the perfect way for the highest expression of my talents. I follow the lead which enters my conscious, reasoning mind."

+ The Guiding Principle can protect you from harm and warn you of impending danger. It can save your life!

+ Divine Right Action comes to you when your motives are right and when you sincerely desire to do right.

+ Feel, believe, claim, and know at all times that you are guided, directed, sustained, and blessed. As you continue to reinforce this truth in your subconscious mind, you will be automatically guided.

+ Come to a clear-cut decision that you were born to succeed and to lead a triumphant and constructive life. Claim and believe the royal road to success is yours now, and the Cosmic Guiding Principle will guide you to victory, triumph, and phenomenal success.

+ To claim the fortune in your mind, call upon the Infinite Intelligence within you to reveal a new creative idea which will bless you and humanity. According to your belief is it done unto you.

+ Cosmic Intelligence is omniscient. It can help you find objects and people. If you are looking for a long-lost relative or friend, affirm boldly, knowing and believing the answer will come, "Cosmic Intelligence knows where this person is and reveals his whereabouts in Divine Order. I release this to the ocean of my subjective mind, and it reveals the answer in its own way."

CHAPTER 13

Perform Miracles in Your Life and the Lives of Others

A miracle cannot prove the impossible. It is a confirmation of that which is, always was, and always will be possible. History provides us with stories of highly spiritual individuals performing miracles—curing the ill, raising the dead, transforming or multiplying physical objects, appearing to the living after death, and so on. However, until now, little guidance has been provided on how to perform miracles. By harnessing the power of your subconscious mind, you, too, will be able to perform miracles.

To believe is to accept something as true. Great numbers of people, however, believe that which is false; consequently, they suffer to the extent of their belief. If, for example, you believe that Los Angeles is in Arizona and you address your letter accordingly, it will go astray or be returned to you. Remember that to accept an idea is to believe it. If someone suggests to you that you were born to succeed, to become victorious over life's problems, and you accept this completely without any mental reservation, apparent miracles will happen in your life!

I say "*apparent* miracles" because nothing is miraculous about the power of the subconscious mind; its function and the outcomes it produces are aligned with natural and supernatural laws. In many ways, the "miracles" that occur are the result of cause and effect: impressing a desire upon the subconscious mind creates the object of that desire in the subjective world of the subconscious, which brings it into being in the objective world, the so-called *real* world.

The Miracle of Implicit Believing

When Alexander the Great, the ancient monarch, was a very young, impressionable boy, his mother, Olympia, told him that his nature was Divine, and that he was different from all other boys, because she had been impregnated by the god Zeus; therefore, he would transcend all the limitations of the average boy. The youth firmly believed this and grew up magnificent in stature, power, and strength; and his life was a series of glorious exploits beyond the comprehension of the average man. He was called "the Divine Lunatic." Alexander was constantly accomplishing both the unpredictable and the impossible. He became an outstanding warrior and conqueror. He accepted completely the belief that he was not the son of his human father, Philip of Macedonia.

It is recorded that at one time he put his arms around a wild, fierce, undisciplined stallion; jumped on it without saddle or bridle; and the horse became as gentle as a lamb. His father and the groom wouldn't dare touch the same horse. However, he believed he was Divine and had power over all animals. He conquered the then known world and established the Alexandrian empire. It is said that he wept because there were no more nations to conquer.

I cite this just to show the power of belief, which enables you to make the so-called impossible possible. Alexander believed, and dramatized his belief to himself, and made manifest in his own way this Infinite Power in his mind, body, and achievement.

Why You Should Know You Are Divine

You are a child of the Living Spirit. You are born Divine. You have the power, ability, and capacity to do godlike things. Think of all the wonderful things you can accomplish as you call on the Infinite Power within you. Your belief that you are at one with Divine Presence will set aside all false human beliefs and opinions and enable you to do Divine works here and now.

Start today to acknowledge your divine nature. Affirm frequently:

> I know and believe I am born of Divine Intelligence and Power, and I am endowed with all Divine Powers, Qualities, and Attributes. I believe implicitly in my Divine nature and I accept my Divine birthright. I am made in the image and likeness of my Creator. I have been given dominion over all things. I can overcome all problems and challenges through the Infinite Power of the Living Spirit within me. Every problem of mine is divinely outmatched. I believe I can release the infinite healing presence to relieve suffering in myself and in others. I am inspired and illumined from on High. I am expressing more and more of Divine Love, Light, Truth, and Beauty every day. I know all things are possible to me because I am Divine. I claim this moment that the Light of the Living Spirit shines in me and Its glory is risen upon me. I can do all things through the Divine Power that strengthens me.

Continue to reiterate these truths until they become a subjective embodiment, and wonders will happen in your life.

Ask yourself, "Does this which I desire exist for me?" Do you believe that you can have wonderful friends and companionship? Do you believe that all the wealth you need is a possibility for you in the universal scheme of things? Do you believe you can find your true place in life? Do you believe that the will of the Living Spirit for you is the abundant life, a greater measure of happiness, peace, joy, prosperity, greater expression, and buoyant health? You should answer all these questions affirmatively and believe and expect the best from life, and the best will come to you.

What Many People Erroneously Believe about Abundance in Their Lives

Many people think that wealth, happiness, and abundance are not for them, but that these are only for others. This is due to a feeling of inferiority or rejection. There is no such thing as an inferior or a superior person. Everyone is part of Divine Nature and has access to Its Infinite Power.

You are not limited by family, background, or early conditioning. Millions of people have transcended their environments and have raised their heads and shoulders above the crowd, although they were not born with gold spoons in their mouths. Abraham Lincoln was born in a log cabin; Jesus was the son of a carpenter; George Washington Carver, the great scientist, was born into slavery. The universal bounty of Divine Abundance, however, is poured out on all regardless of color, creed, or gender, or other differences.

It is done unto you as you believe. If you don't believe that you have the right to your heart's desire, then you are leaving your fate entirely up to chance or what others choose for you.

You Have the Right to Believe in Rich and Joyous Living

Cosmic Goodness gave you richly all things to enjoy, and you are placed here to glorify your Creator and enjoy your abundant blessings. You have the perfect right to bring any good into your life provided your motive is unselfish and that you wish all the best for everyone as you do for yourself. Your desire for health, happiness, peace, love, and abundance cannot possibly harm anyone. You have the right to a wonderful position with a marvelous income, but you should not covet any other person's job. The infinite presence can guide you to right employment with an income consistent with your integrity and honesty.

Believe you have the right to the good you seek and do everything you know to bring it into your experience, and then it will manifest. You don't want anything some other person is enjoying. Divine Infinite Riches are available to all. Life responds to you according to your belief in It and your use of It.

All your experiences, conditions, and events grow out of your beliefs. Cause and effect are indissolubly united and linked together. Your habitual thinking finds its expression in all phases of your life. Believe you have a Silent Partner who comforts you, guides and directs you, and holds before you an open door which nobody can shut. Live in the joyous expectancy of the best, and invariably the best will come to you.

Every morning when you wake, affirm quietly and lovingly:

> This is the day the Lord hath made. I will rejoice and be glad
> in it. Wonders will happen in my life today. I will make marvelous
> contacts today. I will meet wonderful, interesting people. I will
> complete all my assignments in Divine Order, and I will
> accomplish great things today. My Silent Partner reveals to me
> new and better ways to accomplish all things. I know the
> Infinite Power sees no obstacles, knows no barriers. I believe
> the Living Spirit is prospering me beyond my wildest dreams.
> I know and believe that all things are possible to those who
> believe.

How to Help the Poor

Never pity the poor or ruminate over poverty. The poor have never been made rich by thinking about poverty. Health is not restored by focusing on illness. Goodness is not attained by thinking about sin.

The poor do not need charity; they need opportunity and inspiration. As the old saying goes, "Give someone a fish and you feed him for a day; teach someone to fish, and you feed him for a lifetime." Even better, build a business or an industry around a new idea and create wealth and opportunity that feed tens, hundreds, or even thousands of people for a lifetime.

You are not being callous when you refuse to pity the poor or try to solve the poverty problem. You serve the poor and contribute most to solving the poverty problem by steering your thoughts toward prosperity and away from poverty, by thinking yourself and others rich. Jumping into the same hole that the poor have found themselves in does them little good. You can do much more from outside the hole, providing the means for them to climb out on their own. This, too, is a miracle.

How a Bankrupt Man Claimed His Good

Some time ago I interviewed a man who had gone bankrupt. He was depressed and dejected. Furthermore, his wife had divorced him, and his children no longer contacted him. He said that his wife had poisoned their minds against him. He commented that he did not believe in a Divine Being and that he was at the end of the rope.

I pointed out to him that even if he believed the world is flat, nevertheless, it is still round. Furthermore, there is Infinite Intelligence within a person whether he believes there is or not. I suggested to him that he try a formula for ten days, and at the end of that time come back and see me. The formula I gave him was as follows:

> I believe in Divine Being, the Infinite Power that moves the world and created all things. I believe this Infinite Power dwells in me. I believe Divine Intelligence is guiding me now. I believe Divine Riches flow to me in avalanches of abundance. I believe Divine Love fills my heart and that this love fills the minds and hearts of my two boys. I believe that the bonds of love and peace unite us. I believe I am a tremendous success. I believe I am happy, joyous, and free. I believe Divine Being is always successful, and because It is successful and because It dwells in me, I am a tremendous success. I believe, I believe, I believe.

I suggested that he affirm the above truths out loud five minutes morning, afternoon, and night. He agreed, and the second day he phoned and said, "I don't believe a word of what I am saying. It's all mechanical and has no meaning." I told him to persist in this mental discipline. "The mere fact that you started to affirm and practice the spiritual formula indicates that you have at least some degree of faith; and, as you keep it up, you will remove the mountains of doubt, fear, lack, and frustration."

He came back at the end of ten days radiant and happy. His two sons had visited him, and they had a joyous reunion. In his new pattern of thought, he won a small fortune on the Irish Sweepstakes and is now back in business. He discovered that the Infinite Power for Divine living also applied to him!

I knew that even though the words of the prayer meant nothing to him as he started, as he continued to dwell upon them through frequent habitation of the mind, they would sink into his subconscious mind and become a part of his mentality. Even if you are not a believer in religion of any sort, you have the power, through your subconscious mind, to make incredible positive changes in your life. All you need to do is plant the seeds of change in the soil of your subconscious and believe they will take root, sprout, and bear fruit.

Chapter Takeaways

+ To believe is to accept something as true. If you believe a falsehood, you will suffer to the extent of your belief.

+ Like Alexander the Great, if you believe that your nature is Divine, you will be able to accomplish what others believe is impossible.

✦ Believe you can be, do, and have all you desire through Divine Power and Divine Intelligence.

✦ The key to being, doing, and having whatever you desire is faith. Love, joy, serenity, gratitude, kindness, enthusiasm, and other positive feelings are signs of faith. Doubt, fear, anxiety, despair, anger, and other negative emotions are all signs of a lack of faith.

✦ Look beyond appearances and what others may consider impossible and contemplate the reality of the wish fulfilled.

✦ Examine your beliefs and recast them in the light of the great affirmatives. Believe in Divine Power, Divine Guidance, and Divine Abundance.

✦ You are divinely entitled to all the riches of life. Accept your good now and live in the joyous expectancy of the best.

✦ All your experiences and circumstances grow out of your belief. Change your belief, and you will change your reality.

✦ Even if you do not believe in a Higher Power, the mere fact that you begin to affirm the truth is the faith of a grain of mustard seed, which continues to grow as you announce these truths to your mind.

✦ If you harness the power of your subconscious mind as explained in this book, you will soon discover that faith works wonders and even so-called miracles in your life.

CHAPTER 14

Affirmations for Health, Wealth, Relationships, and Self-Fulfillment

◆

Affirmations are very effective for impressing conscious thoughts and desires upon the subconscious mind. They serve two purposes: First, they blot out any negative thoughts, images, and self-talk from the conscious mind. Second, they fill the conscious mind with positive thoughts, images, and self-talk, so they can begin to make an impression upon the subconscious mind.

This chapter is full of powerful affirmations for Health, Wealth, Relationships, and Self-Fulfillment, because growing rich extends beyond money and physical possessions. A life of abundance and prosperity encompasses all aspects of one's life, including health, relationships, and personal fulfillment, all of which support one's ability to prosper financially.

The idea behind affirmations is simple. Most of us grow up learning to put ourselves down for any real or imagined error. We grow up believing certain things about ourselves or comparing ourselves negatively to others. Our minds are filled with self-doubt. By repeating affirmations, we replace self-defeating thoughts with images of empowerment.

Depending on how deeply ingrained our negative beliefs have become, how strongly we believe the affirmation, and how quickly our subconscious responds to our commands, results may be immediate or require some time to unfold. Remain patient and continue to repeat the affirmation one or more times daily with the proper mindset—a firm conviction that what you are saying is true, and a clear image in your mind of having, doing, being that which you desire.

Health

Your DNA contains the blueprint for your body, and your mind controls all bodily functions. Without conscious effort, your heart beats; your lungs take in air; food is digested; nutrients are delivered to the organs and tissues that need them; harmful viruses and bacteria are identified, killed, and eliminated; cuts and bruises are healed.

Illness is the result of the subconscious mind accepting an unhealthy idea or belief. To restore health, the subconscious needs to be reminded of the Life Force in the body that drives healthy form and function. Just as there can be no darkness where there is light, there can be no illness where there is perfect health.

The affirmations in this section help you impress upon your subconscious mind the Divine Perfection that flows through your body, restores health, and makes you whole.

Align with the Infinite Principle of Love and Life

> **The Divine in me has limitless possibilities. I know that all things are possible with the Living Spirit. I believe this and accept it**

wholeheartedly now. I know that the Divine Power in me makes darkness light and crooked things straight. I am now raised in consciousness by contemplating that Divine Being dwells within me.

I speak the word now for the healing of mind, body, and affairs; I know that this Principle within me responds to my faith and trust. I am now in touch with life, love, truth, and beauty within me. I now align myself with the Infinite Principle of Love and Life within me. I know that harmony, health, and peace are now being expressed in my body.

As I live, move, and act in the assumption of my perfect health, it becomes actual. I now imagine and feel the reality of my perfect body. I am filled with a sense of peace, well-being, and gratitude, knowing that as I believe, it is done unto me.

Invoke the Healing Principle

I positively believe in the healing power of the Divine within me. My conscious and subconscious minds are in perfect agreement. I accept the statement of truth which I positively affirm. The words I speak are words of spirit and truth.

I now decree that Divine Healing Power is transforming my whole body, making me whole, pure, and perfect. I believe with a deep, inner certitude that my prayer of faith is being manifest now. I am guided by Divine Wisdom in all matters. Divine Love flows in transcendent beauty and loveliness into my mind and body, transforming, normalizing, and energizing every atom of my being. I sense the peace that surpasses all understanding. Divine Glory surrounds me, and I rest forever in Everlasting Arms.

Wear His Garment

I feel Divine Presence in the sanctuary of my own soul. Divine Being is Life; that Life is my life. I know that Divine Being is not a body; It is shapeless, timeless, and ageless; I see It in my mind's eye. Through understanding, I see and look upon Divine Being in the same way that I see the answer to a mathematical problem.

I now rise to the awareness of peace, poise, and power. This feeling of joy, peace, and goodwill within me is the Living Spirit moving within me. It is Divine Being in action. It is Almighty. There is no power in external things to hurt me; the only Power resides in my own mind and consciousness.

My body is the garment of the Divine. The Living Spirit Almighty is within me. It is pure, holy, and perfect. I know that this Holy Spirit is Divine and that this Spirit is now flowing through me, healing and making my body whole, pure, and perfect. I have complete power over my body and my world.

My thoughts of peace, power, and health have the Power of the Almighty to be realized within me now. I see and feel the Holy presence; it is wonderful.

Quiet Your Mind

Divinity dwells at the center of my being. This Divine Presence is peace, which enfolds me in Its Arms now. A deep feeling of security, vitality, and strength underlie this peace. This inner sense of peace, in which I now dwell, is the silent, brooding Divine Presence. The Love and the Light of the Living Spirit watch over me, as a loving mother watches over her sleeping child. Deep in my heart is the Holy presence that is my peace, my strength, and my source of supply.

All fear has vanished. I see the Divine in all people; I see Divine Being manifest in all things. I am an instrument of the Divine Presence. I now release this inner peace; it flows through my entire being releasing and dissolving all problems; this is the peace that surpasses all understanding.

Gain Mental Poise

I am now full of a Divine Enthusiasm, because I am in the presence of Divinity. I am in the presence of All Power, Wisdom, Majesty, and Love.

The Light of Divine Intelligence illuminates my mind, filling it with poise, balance, and equilibrium. I experience a perfect mental adjustment, aligning myself with the Divine Healing Power. I am at peace with my own thoughts. I rejoice in my work; it gives me joy and happiness. I draw continually upon my Divine Storehouse; for It is the only presence and the only power. My mind is Divine; I am at peace.

Experience Divine Peace

All is peace and harmony in my world, for the Living Spirit in me is the Lord of Peace. I am the consciousness of Divine Being in action; I am always at peace. My mind is poised, serene, and calm. In this atmosphere of peace and goodwill which surrounds me, I feel a deep abiding strength and freedom from all fear. I now sense and feel the love and beauty of His Holy presence. Day by day I am more aware of Divine Love; all that is false falls away. I see Divine Being personified in all people. I know that as I allow this inner peace to flow through my being, all problems are solved. I dwell in the Divine; therefore, I rest in the eternal arms of peace. My peace is the deep, unchanging peace of Divine Being.

Heal with Spiritual Medicine

The spirit of the Almighty pervades every atom of my being, making me whole, joyous, and perfect. I know that all functions of my body respond to this inner joy welling up within me. I am now stirring up the gift of the Living Spirit within me; I feel wonderful. The oil of joy and illumination anoint my intellect and become a lamp unto my feet.

I am now Divinely adjusted emotionally; a Divine Equilibrium governs my mind, body, and affairs. I resolve from this moment forward to express peace and happiness to every person I meet. I know that my happiness and peace come from the Living Spirit; as I shed Its light, love, and truth on others, I am also blessing and healing myself in countless ways. I radiate the sunshine of Divine Love to all humanity. Its light shines through me and illuminates my path. I am resolved to express peace, joy, and happiness.

Control Your Emotions

When a negative thought of fear, jealousy, or resentment enters my mind, I supplant it with Divine Intelligence. My thoughts are Divine Thoughts, and Divine Power is with my thoughts of good. I know I have complete dominion over my thoughts and emotions. I am a channel of the Divine. I now redirect all my feelings and emotions along harmonious, constructive lines. I now rejoice to accept the ideas of Divine Intelligence, which are peace, harmony, and goodwill, and I delight to express them; this heals all discord within me. Only Divine Ideas enter my mind, bringing me harmony, health, and peace.

The Living Spirit is Love. Divine Love casts out fear, resentment, and all negative states. I now fall in love with Truth. I wish for everyone everything I wish for myself; I radiate love, peace, and goodwill to all. I am at peace.

Be One with the Divine Essence Within

I am still and at peace. My heart and my mind are motivated by the spirit of goodness, truth, and beauty. My thought is now on the Divine Presence within me; this stills my mind.

I know that the way of creation is Spirit moving upon itself. My True Self now moves in and on Itself creating peace, harmony, and health in my body and affairs. I am Divine in my deeper self. I know I am a child of the Living Spirit; I create the way my Creator creates, by the self-contemplation of spirit. I know my body does not move of itself. It is acted upon by my thoughts and emotions.

I now say to my body, "Be still and quiet." It must obey. I understand this and I know it is a Divine Law. I take my attention away from the physical world; I feast in the House of the Divine within me. I meditate and feast upon harmony, health, and peace; these come forth from the Divine Essence within; I am at peace. My body is a temple of the Living Spirit.

Wealth

To grow rich, remember and apply these three eternal principles:

+ There is no shortage of supply. What you receive is limited only by your capacity to receive it, not by the supply available.

+ Avoid zero-sum thinking—the mistaken notion that for one person to gain, another must lose. Because there is no

shortage of supply, what others have has nothing to do
with what is available for you. Hence, there is no reason to
be jealous or envious of others.

✦ Be friendly to money. You cannot at the same time desire
money and belittle or look down upon people who have it
or dismiss money as undesirable. The two notions cancel
each other out in the subconscious mind.

The affirmations in this section will help you to develop the
proper mind-set to maximize your capacity to receive the riches
you desire.

Celebrate the Moment

Know that my good is this very moment. I believe in my heart
that I can prophesy for myself harmony, wealth, peace, and joy. I
enthrone the concepts of peace, success, and prosperity in my
mind now. I know and believe these thoughts (seeds) will grow
and manifest themselves in my experience.

I am the gardener; as I sow, so will I reap. I sow Divine
Thoughts (seeds); these wonderful seeds are peace, success, harmony, and goodwill. It is a wonderful harvest.

From this moment forward I am depositing in the Divine
Bank (my subconscious mind) seeds or thoughts of peace, confidence, poise, and balance. I am drawing out the fruit of the
wonderful seeds I am depositing. I believe and accept the fact
that my desire is a seed deposited in the subconscious. I make it
real by feeling the reality of it. I accept the reality of my desire in
the same manner I accept the fact that the seed deposited in the
ground will grow. I know it sprouts in the darkness; also, my

desire or ideal sprouts in the darkness of my subconscious mind; in a little while, like the seed, it comes above the ground (becomes objectified) as a condition, circumstance, or event.

Infinite Intelligence governs and guides me in all ways. I meditate on all things true, honest, just, lovely, and of good report. I think on these things, and Divine Power is with my thoughts of Good. I am at peace.

Identify with the Infinite Source of Supply

I now give a pattern of success and prosperity to the deep mind within me, which is the law. I now identify myself with the Infinite Source of supply. I listen to the still, small voice of Divine Intelligence within me. This inner voice leads, guides, and governs all my activities. I am one with Divine Abundance. I know and believe that there are new and better ways of conducting my business; Infinite Intelligence reveals the new ways to me.

I am growing in wisdom and understanding. My business or profession is Divine Business. I am divinely prospered in all ways. Divine Wisdom within me reveals the ways and means by which all my affairs are adjusted in the right way immediately.

The words of faith and conviction which I now speak open all the necessary doors or avenues for my success and prosperity. My feet are kept on the perfect path, because I am a child of the Living Spirit.

Rejoice in the Abundant Life

I know that *to grow rich* means to grow spiritually along all lines. Divine Intelligence enriches me now in mind, body, and affairs. Divine Ideas constantly unfold within me, bringing to me health, wealth, and perfect Divine Expression.

I thrill inwardly as I feel the Living Spirit vitalizing every atom of my being. I know that Divine Life is animating, sustaining, and strengthening me now. I am now expressing a perfect, radiant body full of vitality, energy, and power.

My business or profession is a Divine Activity, and since it is Divine Business, it is successful and prosperous. I imagine and feel an inner wholeness functioning through my body, mind, and affairs. I give thanks and rejoice in the abundant life.

Engage the Power of Faith

I know that no matter what the negation of yesterday was, my daily affirmation of truth will rise triumphantly over it today. I steadfastly behold the joy of the answered request. I walk all day long in the Light.

Today is a glorious day for me, as it is full of peace, harmony, and joy. My faith in the good is written in my heart and felt as an inward glow. I am absolutely convinced of a Divine Presence and a Divine Law which receive the impress of my desire now, and which irresistibly attract into my experience all the good things my heart desires. I now place all my reliance, faith, and trust in the power and presence of the Living Spirit within me; I am at peace.

I know I am a guest of the Infinite, which is my Host. I hear the invitation of the Almighty saying, *Come unto me all you that labor, and I will give you rest.* I rest in the Living Spirit; all is well.

Believe in a Universe of Abundance

I know that Divine Being is prospering me in all ways. I am now leading the abundant life, because I believe in Divine Abundance. I am supplied with everything that contributes to my beauty, well-being, progress, and peace. I am daily experiencing the fruits of the Living Spirit within me; I accept my good now; I walk in the Truth that all good is mine. I am peaceful, poised, serene, and calm. I am one with The Source of life; all my needs are met at every moment of time and every point of space. I now bring all the empty vessels to the Living Spirit that dwells within. Divine Abundance is made manifest in all departments of my life. All that my Creator has is mine. I rejoice that this is so.

Engage Your Imagination

I desire to know more of my Creator and the way It works. My vision is for perfect peace and prosperity for all. I believe the Spirit guides and inspires me now in all ways. I know and believe that the Divine Power within me carries out my directive; this is a deep conviction within me.

I know that imagination is the result of what I conceive in my mind. I make it my daily practice to imagine only for myself and others that which is noble, wonderful, and Divine. I now imagine that I am doing the thing I long to do; I imagine that I now possess the things I long to possess; I imagine I am what I long to be. To make it real, I feel the reality of it; I know and am grateful that it is so.

Solve Business Problems

I know and believe my business is Divine Business; the All-Powerful One is my partner in all my affairs; Its light, love, truth, and inspiration fill my mind and heart in all ways. I solve all my problems by placing my complete trust in the Divine Power within me. I know that this Divine Presence sustains everything. I now rest in security and peace. This day I am surrounded by perfect understanding; there is a Divine Solution to all my problems. I understand everyone; I am understood. I know that all my business relationships are in accord with the Divine Law of Harmony. I know that the Divine dwells in all my customers and clients. I work harmoniously with others to the end that happiness, prosperity, and peace reign supreme.

Receive Divine Compensation

My business is Divine Business. I am always about Divine Business, which is to radiate life, love, and truth to all humanity. I am expressing myself fully now; I am giving of my talents in a wonderful way. I am divinely compensated.

Divine Being is prospering my business, profession, or activity in a wonderful way. I claim that everyone in my organization is a spiritual link driving its growth, welfare, and prosperity; I know this, believe it, and rejoice that it is so. Everyone connected with me is divinely prospered and illumined by the Light.

The Light that shines on and through everyone leads and guides me in all ways. All my decisions are controlled by Divine Wisdom. Infinite Intelligence reveals better ways in which I can serve humanity. I rest in Divine Peace and Harmony.

Claim Success

I know that my business, profession, or activity is Divine Business. Divine Business is always successful. I am growing in wisdom and understanding every day. I know, believe, and accept the fact that Divine Abundance is always working for me, through me, and all around me.

My business or profession is full of right action and right expression. The ideas, money, merchandise, and contacts I need are mine always. All these things are irresistibly attracted to me by the law of attraction. Divine Being is the life of my business; I am divinely guided and inspired in all ways. Every day I am presented with wonderful opportunities to grow, expand, and progress. I am building up goodwill. I am a great success, because I do business with others as I would have them do it with me.

Abide in the Silence

I know and realize that Divine Being is a spirit moving within me. I recognize It as a feeling or deep conviction of harmony and peace within me; It is the movement of my own heart. The spirit or feeling of confidence and faith which now possesses me is the Living Spirit and Its movement across the waters of my mind; this is Divine Being—the Creative Power within me.

I live, move, and have my being in the faith and confidence that goodness, truth, and beauty will follow me all the days of my life; this faith in Supreme Being and all things good is omnipotent; it removes all barriers.

I now close the door of the senses; I withdraw all attention from the world. I turn within to the One, the Beautiful, and the Good; here, I dwell in Divine Being beyond time and space; here, I live, move, and dwell in the shadow of the Almighty. I am free from all fear, from the verdict of the world, and the appearance of things. I accept and embrace Infinite Abundance, the source of the answered request.

I become that which I contemplate. I now feel that I am what I want to be and I possess everything I imagine and claim to be mine. This feeling or awareness is the action of the Divine in me; it is the Creative Power. I give thanks for the joy of the answered request, and I rest in the silence that *It is done.*

Be, Do, and Have

> At the center of my being is Peace; this is Divine Peace. In this stillness I feel strength, guidance, and Divine Presence. I am divinely active; I am expressing the fullness of the Living Spirit along all lines. I am a channel for the Divine, and I now release the imprisoned splendor that is within. I am divinely guided to my true expression in life; I am compensated in a wonderful way. I see Divine Being in everything and personified in everyone everywhere. I know as I permit this river of peace to flow through my being, all my problems are solved, all my needs are met, all my desires are fulfilled. All things I need to fully express myself are irresistibly attracted to me by the Divine Law of attraction. The way is revealed to me; I am full of joy and harmony.

Relationships

The Divine Law of attraction is a concept born out of the New Thought movement. It is the belief that positive or negative thoughts imprinted on the subconscious through the energy of positive or negative emotion deliver corresponding positive or negative results in the real world. This law applies to everything we are, do, and have, including relationships.

To attract the right individuals into your life—a friend, companion, business partner, teacher, mentor, and so on—you simply need to form a clear mental image of the qualities of the person you would like to attract and then infuse it with positive emotion—the feeling that the desired person has arrived. Your subconscious working through the Divinity that flows through all things, seen and unseen, brings the two of you together.

The affirmations in this section bring your subconscious in harmony with the Divinity that flows through all of us to attract the people you desire and those who are best suited to you both, your mutual needs, and what you have to offer one another.

Tune In to the Creator's Broadcast

I always bring harmony, peace, and joy into every situation and into all my personal relationships. I know, believe, and claim that Divine Peace reigns supreme in the mind and heart of everyone in my home and business. No matter what the problem is, I always maintain peace, poise, patience, and wisdom. I fully and freely forgive everyone, regardless of what they may have said or done. I cast all my burdens on the Divine Presence within; I go free; this is a marvelous feeling. I know that blessings come to me as I forgive.

I see the angel of Divine Presence behind every problem or difficult situation. I know the solution is there and that everything is working out in Divine Order. I trust the Divine Presence implicitly; It has the *know-how* to accomplish. The Absolute Order of Heaven and Its Absolute Wisdom are acting through me now and always; I know that order is Heaven's first law.

My mind is now fixed joyously and expectantly on this perfect harmony. I know the result is the inevitable, perfect solution; my answer is Divine, for it is the melody of the Creator's broadcast.

Experience Spiritual Rebirth

Today I am reborn spiritually. I completely detach myself from the old way of thinking, and I bring Divine Love, Light, and Truth into my experience. I consciously feel love for everyone I meet. Mentally I say to everyone I contact, "I see the Divine in you, and I know you see the Divine in me." I recognize the qualities of Divine Being in everyone. I practice this morning, noon, and night; it is a living part of me.

I am reborn spiritually now, because all day long I practice Divine Presence. No matter what I am doing—whether I am walking the street, shopping, or going about my daily business— whenever my thought wanders from good, I bring it back to the contemplation of Divine Presence. I feel noble and dignified. I walk in a high mood sensing my oneness with the Living Spirit. Divine Peace fills my soul.

Liberate Yourself with Love

The Supreme Being is Love and Life; this Life is one and indivisible. Life manifests itself in and through all people. It is at the center of my own being.

I know that light dispels the darkness, so does the love of the good overcome all evil. My knowledge of the power of Love overcomes all negative conditions now. Love and hate cannot dwell together. I now turn Divine Light upon all fear or anxious thoughts in my mind, and they flee. The dawn (light of truth) appears and the shadows (fear and doubt) flee.

I know Divine Love watches over me, guides me, and clears the path for me. I am expanding into the Divine. I am now expressing the Divine in all my thoughts, words, and actions; the nature of the Divine is Love. I know that *Divine Love eliminates all fear.*

The Secret Place

I dwell in the secret place of the Most High; this is my own mind. All my thoughts conform to harmony, peace, and goodwill. My mind is the dwelling place of happiness, joy, and a deep sense of security. All thoughts that enter my mind contribute to my joy, peace, and general welfare. I live, move, and have my being in the atmosphere of good fellowship, love, and unity.

All the people who dwell in my mind are Divine. I am at peace in my mind with all the members of my household and all humanity. The same good I wish for me, I wish for all men. I am living in the house of Divine Being now. I claim peace and happiness, for I know I dwell in this house forever.

Control Your Emotions

I am always poised, serene, and calm. Divine Peace floods my mind and my whole being. I practice the Golden Rule and sincerely wish peace and goodwill to everyone.

I know that the love of all things good penetrates my mind casting out all fear. I am now living in the joyous expectancy of the best. My mind is free from all worry and doubt. My words of truth now dissolve every negative thought and emotion within me. I forgive everyone; I open the doorway of my heart to Divine Presence. My whole being is flooded with the light and understanding from within.

The petty things of life no longer irritate me. When fear, worry, and doubt knock at my door, faith in goodness, truth, and beauty open the door, and there is no one there.

Express Your Gratitude

I give thanks sincerely and humbly for all goodness, truth, and beauty which flow through me. I have a grateful, uplifted heart for all good that has come to me in mind, body, and affairs. I radiate love and goodwill to all humanity. I lift them up in my thought and feeling. I always show my gratitude and give thanks for all my blessings. The grateful heart brings my mind and heart in intimate union with the creative Power of the Cosmos. My thankful and exalted state of mind leads me along the ways by which all good things come.

✳ Attract Your Divine Companion

I know and believe there is a man/woman waiting to love and cherish me. I know I can contribute to his/her happiness and peace. He/she loves my ideals, and I love his/her ideals. He/she does not want to make me over; neither do I want to make him/her over. There is mutual love, freedom, and respect.

There is one mind; I know him/her now in this mind. I unite now with the qualities and attributes that I admire and want expressed by my husband/wife/companion. I am one with them in my mind. We know and love each other already in Divine Mind. I see the Divine in him/her, and he/she sees the Divine in me. Having met within, we must meet in the *without*, for this is the law of my own mind.

These words go forth and accomplish where they are sent. I know it is now done, finished, and accomplished. Thank you.

Attract a Spiritual Companion

Supreme Being is one and indivisible. In It we love, move, and have our being. I know and believe that the Divine dwells in every person; I am one with Divine Being and with all people. I now attract the right person who is in complete accord with me.

I now decree that this person possesses the following qualities and attributes—that he or she is spiritual, loyal, faithful, prosperous, peaceful, and happy. We are irresistibly attracted to each other. Only that which belongs to love, truth, and wholeness can enter my experience. I accept my ideal companion now.

Gain Peace through Unity of Spirit

Peace begins with me. Divine Peace fills my mind; the spirit of goodwill goes forth from me to all humanity. Divine Being is everywhere and fills the hearts of all. In absolute truth, all people are now spiritually perfect; they are expressing Divine Qualities and Attributes. These qualities and attributes are Love, Light, Truth, and Beauty.

There are no separate nations. All people belong to the One Country—the One Nation which is a part of all Divine Creation. A country is a dwelling place; I dwell in the secret place of the Most High; I walk and talk with my Creator; so do all people everywhere. There is only One Divine Family, and that is humanity.

There are no frontiers or barriers between nations, because Divine Being is One; It is indivisible and cannot be divided against Itself. Divine Love permeates the hearts of everyone everywhere. Divine Wisdom rules and guides the nation; It inspires our leaders and the leaders of all nations to do Its will, and Its will only. Divine Peace which passes all understanding fills my mind and the minds of all people throughout the cosmos. Thank you for Your peace; it is done.

Self-Fulfillment

Through the power of the subconscious mind and the Divinity that permeates all things, you are master of your own destiny. You need only develop a clear mental image of the person you want to be and the acts you wish to perform, then use positive emotion, such as acceptance, gratitude, and eager anticipation, to transfer that image to the screen of your subconscious mind. Your subconscious mind will then find a way to reflect that image in objective reality.

Unfortunately, this technique works for negative thoughts and emotions as well, so be careful. If your conscious mind conjures up a clear image of anything negative, and that image becomes energized by negative emotion, such as fear or anxiety, your subconscious mind, having accepted the image, will find a way to reflect it into objective reality as well.

Affirmations play a key role in eradicating negative thoughts, populating your mind with positive images, and energizing those images with positive emotion. This section features several affirmations that enable you to achieve your full potential in any endeavors you choose to pursue.

Take Control

I know that my faith in the Supreme Being determines my future. My faith means my faith in all things good. I unite myself now with true ideas, and I know the future will be in the image and likeness of my habitual thinking. *As a person thinks in his heart so is she.* From this moment forward my thoughts are on: "Whatever things are true, whatever things are honest, whatever things are just, whatever things are lovely and of good report"; day and night I meditate on these things, and I know these seeds (thoughts) which I habitually dwell upon will become a rich harvest for me. I am the captain of my own soul; I am the master of my fate; for my thought and feeling are my destiny.

Define Your Own Destiny

I know that I mold, fashion, and create my own destiny. My faith is my destiny; this means an abiding faith in all things good. I live in the expectancy of the best; only the best comes to me. I know the harvest I will reap in the future, because all my thoughts are Divine Thoughts, thus they are good thoughts. My thoughts are the seeds of goodness, truth, and beauty. I now place my thoughts of love, peace, joy, success, and goodwill in the garden of my mind. This is the Creator's garden, and it will yield an abundant harvest. The glory and beauty of the Divine will be expressed in my life. From this moment forward, I express life, love, and truth. I am radiantly happy and prosperous in all ways. Thank you.

Overcome Fear

There is no fear, as Divine Love expels all fear. Today I permit Love to keep me in perfect harmony and peace with all levels of my world. My thoughts are loving, kind, and harmonious. I sense my oneness with Divine Being, for *in It, I live, move, and have my being.*

I know that all my desires will be realized in perfect order. I trust the Divine Law within me to bring my ideals to pass. *The Living Spirit does the work.* I am divine, spiritual, joyous, and fearless. I am now surrounded by the perfect peace of the Living Spirit. I now place all my attention on the thing desired. I love this desire, and I give it my wholehearted attention.

My spirit is lifted into the mood of confidence and peace; this is the Living Spirit moving in me. It gives me a sense of peace, security, and rest.

Engage Your Imagination

My mind is Divine Mind, and my thoughts are Divine Thoughts. This is how I use my imagination daily: I constantly meditate on whatsoever things are true, honest, just, lovely, and of good report; my imagination is the workshop of the Creator. I imagine only peace, harmony, health, wealth, perfect expression, and love. I reject everything that is not Divine or perfect.

Today I claim my true place. I make it a daily practice to seek first this place within me. I know that this place already exists and will be revealed to me in due time. All my faith is in the Supreme Being and Goodness. Divine Love is supreme in me and casts out all fear. I am at peace. I thank You.

Maintain a Balanced Mind

I know that the inner desires of my heart come from the Living Spirit within me, who wants me to be happy. Divine Will for me is life, love, truth, and beauty. I mentally accept my good now, and I become a perfect, free, flowing channel for the Divine.

I come into Divine Presence singing; I enter Its courts with praise; I am joyful and happy; I am still and poised.

The still small voice whispers in my ear revealing to me my perfect answer. I am a Divine expression. I am always in my true place doing the thing I love to do. I refuse to accept the opinions of others as truth without challenging these opinions with the Eternal Truths I know. I now turn within, and I sense and feel the rhythm of the Divine. I hear the melody of the Living Spirit whispering its message of love to me.

My mind is Divine Mind, and I am always reflecting Divine Wisdom and Divine Intelligence. My brain thinks wisely and spiritually. Divine Ideas unfold within my mind with perfect sequence. I am always poised, balanced, serene, and calm, for I know that Divine Intelligence always reveals to me the perfect solution to all my needs.

Align Yourself with Divine Will

Divine Will for me is goodness, harmony, and abundance. I am now enlightened by the truth; each day I am growing in wisdom and understanding. I am a perfect channel for Divine Being and Intelligence; I am free from all worry and confusion. Infinite Intelligence within me is a lamp that guides my way. I know I am led to do what is right and good, for it is Divine Being in action in all my affairs.

The peace that surpasses all understanding fills my mind now. I believe and accept my ideal. I know it subsists in the Infinite. I give it form and expression by my complete mental acceptance. I feel the reality of the fulfilled desire. Divine Peace fills my soul.

Utter the Creative Word

My creative word is my silent conviction any ideas I plant in my subconscious mind will bear fruit in my life. When I speak the word for healing, success, or prosperity, my word is spoken in the consciousness of Life and Power, knowing that it is done. My word has power, because it is one with Omnipotence. The words I speak are always constructive and creative. When I recite affirmations, my words are full of life, love, and feeling; this makes my thoughts and words creative. I know the greater my faith behind the words spoken, the more power they have. The words I use form a definite mold, which determines what form my thought is to take. Divine Intelligence operates through me now and reveals to me what I need to know. I have the answer now. I am at peace. Divine Being is Peace.

Know That Your Problems Are Solved

I now take my attention away from the problem, whatever it may be. My mind and heart are open to the influx from on High. I know the Kingdom of Heaven is within me. I sense, feel, understand, and know that my own life, my awareness of being, my own *I Am-ness*, is the Living Spirit Almighty. I now turn in recognition to this One Who Forever Is; Divine Light illuminates my pathway; I am divinely inspired and governed in all ways. Now I begin to think and imagine scientifically in order to bring my desire into manifestation by claiming and feeling myself to be, to do, and to have all I desire. I walk in the inner silent knowing of the soul, as I feel the reality of my problem already solved in my heart. Thank You; it is done!

Listen to the Divine Answer

I know that the answer to my problem lies in the Divine within me. I now get quiet, still, and relaxed. I am at peace. I know that the Living Spirit speaks in peace and not in confusion. I am now in tune with the Infinite; I know and believe implicitly that Infinite Intelligence is revealing to me the perfect answer. I think about the solution to my problems. I now live in the mood I would have were my problem solved. I truly live in this abiding faith and trust which is the mood of the solution; this is the Living Spirit moving within me. This Spirit is Omnipotent. It is manifesting Itself. My whole being rejoices in the solution; I am glad. I live in this feeling and give thanks.

I know that Divine Intelligence has the answer. With the Almighty, all things are possible. The Living Spirit Almighty resides within me; It is the Source of all wisdom and illumination.

The indicator of the Divine Presence within me is a sense of peace and poise. I now cease all sense of strain and struggle; I trust the Divine Power implicitly. I know that all the Wisdom and Power I need to live a glorious and successful life are within me. I relax my entire body; I cast all burdens on Divine Power; I go free. I claim and feel Divine Peace flooding my mind, heart, and entire being. I know the quiet mind solves all problems. I now turn my request over to Divine Intelligence, knowing It has an answer. I am at peace.

Experience Divine Freedom

I know the truth, and the truth is that the realization of my desire will free me from all sense of bondage. I accept my freedom; I know it is already established in the creative world of my subconscious mind.

I know that everything I am, have, and experience are projections of my inner attitudes. I am transforming my mind by dwelling on all things true, lovely, noble, and Divine. I contemplate myself now as possessing all the good things of Life, such as harmony, health, wealth, and happiness.

My contemplation rises to the point of acceptance; I accept the desires of my heart completely. Divine Being is the only presence. I am expressing the fullness of the Living Spirit now. I am free! Divine Peace governs my home, heart, and all my affairs.

Seek Divine Guidance

I now dwell on Divine Omnipresence and Omnipotence. I know that this Infinite Wisdom guides the planets on their course. I know this same Divine Intelligence governs and directs all my affairs. I claim and believe Divine Understanding is mine always. I know that all my activities are controlled by this presence dwelling in me. All my motives are Divine and true. Divine Wisdom, Truth, and Beauty are being expressed through me always. The All-Knowing One within me knows what to do and how to do it. My life is governed by the love of the Supreme Being. Divine Guidance is mine. I know the answer, for my mind is at peace. I rest in Everlasting Arms.

Commit to Right Action

I radiate goodwill to all humanity in thought, word, and deed. I know the peace and goodwill that I radiate to others come back to me a thousandfold. Whatever I need to know comes to me from the Divine Intelligence within me. Divine Intelligence is operating through me, revealing to me what I need to know. It knows the answer. The perfect answer is made known to me now. Infinite Intelligence and Divine Wisdom make all decisions through me, and only right action and right expression are taking place in my life. Every night I wrap myself in the Divine Mantle of Love and fall asleep knowing Divine Guidance is mine. When the dawn comes, I am filled with peace. I go forth into the new day full of faith, confidence, and trust. Thank You.

Resurrect Your Desire

My desire for health, harmony, peace, abundance, and security is the voice of the Living Spirit speaking to me. I choose to be happy and successful. I am guided in all ways. I open my mind and heart to the influx of Divine Intelligence; I am at peace. I draw successful and happy people into my experience. I recognize only the Divine Presence and Power within me.

The light of the Living Spirit shines through me and from me into everything about me. The emanation of Divine Love flows from me. It is a healing radiance unto everyone who comes into my Divine Presence.

I now assume the feeling of being what I want to be. I know that the way to resurrect my desire is to remain faithful to my ideal, knowing that an Almighty Power is working on my behalf. I live in this mood of faith and confidence; I give thanks that it is done; for it has already taken shape in the workshop of my subconscious mind, and all is well.

Achieve Your Goal

My knowledge of Divine Being and the way It works is growing by leaps and bounds. I control and direct all my emotions along peaceful, constructive channels. Divine Love fills all my thoughts, words, and actions. My mind is at peace; I am at peace with all people. I am always relaxed and at ease. I know that I am here to express my inner Divinity fully in all ways. I believe implicitly in the guidance of the Divine Intelligence within me. This Infinite Intelligence reveals to me the perfect plan of expression; I move toward it confidently and joyously. The goal and the objective I have in my mind are good and very good. I have planted in my mind the way of fulfillment. Divine Power now moves in my behalf and illumines my path.

Infinite Intelligence reveals better ways in which I can serve humanity. I rest in Divine Peace and Harmony.

Solve Your Problems

I know that a problem has its solution within it in the form of a desire. The realization of my desire is good and very good. I know and believe that the Creative Power within me has the absolute Power to bring forth that which I deeply desire. The Principle which gave me the desire is the Principle which gives it birth. About this, I am certain.

I now ride the white horse which is the Living Spirit moving across the waters of my mind. I take my attention away from the problem and dwell upon the reality of the fulfilled desire. I am following Divine Law now. I assume the feeling that whatever I desire and believe is delivered. I make it real by the feeling of being, having, or doing it. In Divine Wisdom I live, move, and have my being; I live in this feeling and give thanks.

Lead the Triumphant Life

I now let go of everything; I enter the realization of peace, harmony, and joy. The Supreme Being is over all, through all, and in all. I lead the triumphant life, because I know that Divine Love guides, directs, sustains, and heals me. Divine Presence is the very core of my being. It is made manifest now in every atom of my body. There can be no delay, impediment, or obstruction to the realization of my heart's desire. Divine Omnipotence is now moving on my behalf. *Nothing and no one can stop It.* I know what I want; my desire is clear-cut and definite. I accept it completely in my mind. I remain faithful to the end. I have entered the house of the Living Spirit, and my mind is at peace.

Source Notes

✦

The writings in this book were collected or adapted from books, booklets, speeches, and lectures by Joseph Murphy. In some cases, new material has been added to further illuminate the significance for the modern reader, at the discretion of the Joseph Murphy Trust. Primary sources are listed below.

Joseph Murphy. 2005. *Maximize Your Potential Through the Power of Your Subconscious Mind to Create Wealth and Success*

J. Murphy. 1969. *Infinite Power for Richer Living*

J. Murphy. 1952. *A Guide to Your Healing Powers*

Lectures
- Adjusting to Wealth and Health
- Building Self-Confidence
- Realize Your Desire
- Three Steps to Success
- The Master Key to Wealth
- Programming Your Subconscious
- The Wonders of Master Thought
- High Vision Leads to High Places
- How to Think with Authority

Booklets

Joseph Murphy. 1946. "Getting Results"

J. Murphy. 1949. "How to Prosper"

J. Murphy. 1948. "Riches Are Your Right"

J. Murphy. 1973. "Steps to Success"

Acknowledgments

✦

To our team at Penguin Random House, Marian Lizzi, Rachel Ayotte, and others, for acknowledging the deep desire from readers for Joseph Murphy's books and keeping Joseph Murphy relevant for new generations of readers. Thank you for guiding us through the process.

Grateful acknowledgment is made to Joe Kraynak, editor in chief, for his knowledge of and passion for Joseph Murphy's philosophy. Joe's skills and professionalism are unsurpassed.

About the Author

◆

Dr. Joseph Murphy was born on May 20, 1898, in a small town in County Cork, Ireland. His father, Denis Murphy, was a deacon and professor at the National School of Ireland, a Jesuit facility. His mother, Ellen, née Connelly, was a housewife, who later gave birth to another son, John, and a daughter, Catherine.

Joseph was brought up in a strict Catholic household. His father was quite devout and, indeed, was one of the few lay professors who taught Jesuit seminarians. He had a broad knowledge of many subjects and developed in his son the desire to study and learn.

Ireland at that time was suffering from one of its many economic depressions, and many families were starving. Although Denis Murphy was steadily employed, his income was barely enough to sustain the family.

Young Joseph was enrolled in the National School and was a brilliant student. He was encouraged to study for the priesthood and was accepted as a Jesuit seminarian. However, by the time he reached his late teen years, he began to question the Catholic orthodoxy of the Jesuits, and he withdrew from the seminary. Since his goal was to explore new ideas and gain new experiences—a goal he could not pursue in Catholic-dominated Ireland—he left his family to go to America.

He arrived at the Ellis Island immigration center with only five dollars in his pocket. His first project was to find a place to live. He was fortunate to locate a rooming house where he shared a room with a pharmacist who worked in a local drugstore.

Joseph's knowledge of English was minimal, as Gaelic was spoken both in his home and at school, so like most Irish immigrants, Joseph worked as a day laborer, earning enough to keep fed and housed.

He and his roommate became good friends, and when a job opened up at the drugstore where his friend worked, he was hired to be an assistant to the pharmacist. He immediately enrolled in a school to study pharmacy. With his keen mind and desire to learn, it didn't take long before Joseph passed the qualification exams and became a full-fledged pharmacist. He now made enough money to rent his own apartment. After a few years, he purchased the drugstore, and for the next few years ran a successful business.

When the United States entered World War II, Joseph enlisted in the army and was assigned to work as a pharmacist in the medical unit of the 88th Infantry Division. At that time, he renewed his interest in religion and began to read extensively about various religious beliefs. After his discharge from the army, he chose not to return to his career in pharmacy. He traveled extensively, taking courses in several universities both in the United States and abroad.

From his studies, Joseph became enraptured by the various Asian religions and went to India to learn about them in depth. He studied all the major religions from the time of their beginning. He extended these studies to the great philosophers from ancient times until the present.

Although he studied with some of the most intelligent and farsighted professors, the one person who most influenced Joseph was Dr. Thomas Troward, who was a judge as well as a philosopher, doctor, and professor. Judge Troward became Joseph's mentor. From him he not only learned philosophy, theology, and law, but also was introduced to mysticism and, particularly, the Masonic order. He became an active member of this order and over the years rose in the Masonic ranks to the 32nd degree in the Scottish Rite.

Upon his return to the United States, Joseph chose to become a minister and bring his broad knowledge to the public. As his concept of Christianity was not traditional and indeed ran counter to most of the Christian denominations, he founded his own church in Los Angeles. He attracted a small number of congregants, but it did not take long for his message of optimism and hope, rather than the "sin and damnation" sermons of so many ministers, to attract many men and women to his church.

Dr. Joseph Murphy was a proponent of the New Thought movement. This movement was developed in the late nineteenth and early twentieth centuries by many philosophers and deep thinkers who studied this phenomenon and preached, wrote, and practiced a new way of looking at life. By combining a metaphysical, spiritual, and pragmatic approach to the way we think and live, they uncovered the secret of attaining what we truly desire.

The proponents of the New Thought movement preached a new idea of life that brings out new methods and better outcomes, and that we have the power to use these methods to enrich our lives. We can do all these things only as we have found the law and worked out the understanding of the law, which God seemed to have written in riddles in the past.

Of course, Dr. Murphy wasn't the only minister to preach this positive message. Several churches, whose ministers and congregants were influenced by the New Thought movement, were founded and developed in the decades following World War II. The Church of Religious Science, the Unity Church, and similar places of worship preach philosophies similar to this. Dr. Murphy named his organization "The Church of Divine Science." He often shared platforms, conducted joint programs with his similar-thinking colleagues, and trained other men and women to join their ministry.

Over the years, other churches joined with him in developing an organization called the Federation of Divine Science, which acts as an umbrella for all Divine Science churches. Each of the Divine Science church leaders continues to push for more education, and Dr. Murphy was one of the leaders to support the creation of the Divine Science School in St. Louis, Missouri, to train new ministers and provide ongoing education for both ministers and congregants.

The annual meeting of the Divine Science ministers was a must to attend, and Dr. Murphy was a featured speaker at them. He encouraged the participants to study and continue to learn, particularly about the importance of the subconscious mind.

Over the next few years, Murphy's local Church of Divine Science grew so large that his building was too small to hold the congregation. He rented the Wilshire Ebell Theatre, a former movie theater. His services were so well attended that even this venue could not always accommodate all who wished to attend. Classes conducted by Dr. Murphy and his staff supplemented his Sunday services that were attended by 1,300 to 1,500 people. These were supplemented by seminars and lectures that were held most days and evenings. The church remained at the Wilshire Ebell Theatre in Los Angeles until 1976, when it moved to a new location in Laguna Hills, California, near a retirement community.

To reach the vast numbers of people who wanted to hear his message, Dr. Murphy created a weekly radio talk show, which eventually reached an audience of over a million listeners.

Many of his followers wanted more than just summaries and suggested that he tape his lectures and radio programs. He was at first reluctant to do so but agreed to experiment. His radio programs were recorded on extra-large 78 rpm discs, a common practice at that time. He had six cassettes made from one of these discs and placed them on the information table in the lobby of the Wilshire Ebell Theatre. They sold out the first hour. This started a new venture. The tapes of his lectures explaining biblical texts and providing meditations and prayers for his listeners were sold not only in his church, but in other churches, bookstores, and via mail.

As the church grew, Dr. Murphy added a staff of professional and administrative personnel to assist him in the many programs in which he was involved and in researching and preparing his first books. One of the most effective members of his staff was his administrative secretary, Dr. Jean Wright. The working relationship developed into a romance, and they were married—a lifelong partnership that enriched both of their lives.

At this time (the 1950s), there were very few major publishers of spiritually inspired material. The Murphys located some small publishers in the Los Angeles area, and with them produced a series of small books (often thirty to fifty pages printed in pamphlet form) that were sold, mostly in churches, from $1.50 to $3.00 per book. When the orders for these books increased to the point where they required second and third printings, major publishers recognized that there was a market for such books and added them to their catalogs.

Dr. Murphy became well known outside of the Los Angeles area as a result of his books, tapes, and radio broadcasts and was invited to lecture all over the country. He did not limit his lectures to religious matters, but spoke on the historical values of life, the art of wholesome living, and on the teachings of great philosophers—both from the Western and Oriental cultures.

As Dr. Murphy never learned to drive, he had to arrange for somebody to drive him to the various places where he was invited to lecture and other places in his very busy schedule. One of Jean's functions as his administrative secretary and later as his wife was to schedule his assignments and handle his travel arrangements.

The Murphys traveled frequently to many countries around the world. One of his favorite working vacations was to hold seminars on cruise ships. These trips were for a week or more and would take him to many countries.

One of Dr. Murphy's most rewarding activities was speaking to the inmates at many prisons. Many ex-convicts wrote him over the years, telling him how his words had truly turned their lives around and inspired them to live spiritual and meaningful lives.

He toured the United States and many countries in Europe and Asia. In his lectures, he emphasized the importance of understanding the power of the subconscious mind and the life principles based on belief in the one God, the "I Am."

Dr. Murphy's pamphlet-sized books were so popular that he began to expand them into more detailed and longer works. His wife gave us some insight into his manner and method of writing. She reported that he wrote his manuscripts on a tablet and pressed so hard on his pencil or pen that you could read the page by the imprint on the next page. He seemed to be in a trance while writing. His writing style was to remain in his office for four to six hours without disturbance until he stopped and said that was enough for the day. Each day was the same. He never went back into the office again until the next morning to finish what he'd started. He took no food or drink while he was working. He was just alone with his thoughts and his huge library of books, to which he referred from time to time. His wife sheltered him from visitors and calls and kept things moving for church business and other activities.

Dr. Murphy was always looking for a simple way to discuss the issues and to elaborate points that would explain in detail how the individual is affected. He chose some of his lectures to present on cassettes, records, or CDs, as the technologies developed and new methods entered the audio field.

His entire work of CDs and cassettes are tools that can be used to solve most problems that individuals encounter in life and have been time-tested to accomplish the goals as intended. His basic theme is that the solution to every problem lies within oneself. Outside elements cannot change one's thinking. That is, your mind is your own. To live a better life, it's your mind, not outside circumstances, that you must change. You create your own reality and are the master of your destiny. The power of change is in your mind, and by using the power of your subconscious mind, you can make those changes for the better.

Dr. Murphy wrote more than thirty books. His most famous work, *The Power of Your Subconscious Mind*, which was first published in 1963, became an immediate best seller. It was acclaimed as one of the best self-help guides ever written. Millions of copies have been sold and continue to be sold all over the world.

Among some of his other best-selling books were *Telepsychics: The Magic Power of Perfect Living*; *The Amazing Laws of Cosmic Mind Power*; *Secrets of the I Ching*; *The Miracle of Mind Dynamics*; *Your Infinite Power to Be Rich*; and *The Cosmic Power Within You*.

Dr. Murphy died in December 1981, and his wife, Dr. Jean Murphy, continued his ministry after his death. In a lecture she gave in 1986, quoting her late husband, she reiterated his philosophy:

I want to teach men and women of their Divine Origin, and the powers regnant within them. I want to inform that this power is within and that they are their own saviors and capable of achieving their own salvation. This is the message of the Bible, and nine-tenths of our confusion today is due to wrongful, literal interpretation of the life-transforming truths offered in it.

I want to reach the majority, the man on the street, the woman overburdened with duty and suppression of her talents

and abilities. I want to help others at every stage or level of consciousness to learn of the wonders within.

She said of her husband: "He was a practical mystic, possessed by the intellect of a scholar, the mind of a successful executive, the heart of the poet." His message summed up was: "You are the king, the ruler of your world, for you are one with God."